Get **It,** Before **It** Gets You

Author: Kelly L. Shaw

Get **It,** Before **It** Gets You

ISBN-13: **978-0615492551**
Copyright © May 2011
By Holam Books & Media
First Edition

Holam Publishing
www.holambooks.com

Contents

Acknowledgements

First and foremost, I thank and praise my Lord and Savior Jesus Christ. I acknowledge that I couldn't have done this without Him. All Glory and Honor belong to Him. I recognize that it is only through the power and leading of His Spirit that I am able to write anything. God, I am grateful for Your unconditional love even when I was in rebellion, rejecting Your will and Your way. I am thankful for Your hand that was and still is constantly on me, refusing to allow me to settle for less than Your best. Thank you, God for not only Your love but also Your hand of correction that led me in the right direction. I am continuously appreciative for all that You have done and continue to do in my life and the lives of others. Thank you Jesus for confronting my **It** and loving me through my **It** but most of all I thank You for dying on the cross on Calvary. Lord I thank You for once again, choosing me to minister to Your people.

I sincerely appreciate and give thanks to my husband and pastor for his love, patience, support and hard work. I thank you for your teaching and your constant reminders of the importance of reading and following God's word. I also thank God for my Liberty Hill Baptist Church family for their continuous prayers, encouragement and support

In addition a special thanks goes out to Anita Dawson
for all our talks and her continued encouragement
and support. A special thanks to Aqua Groves who
always find a way to keep me laughing. I am
appreciative and thankful for Bishop Timothy Clark
for teaching me the importance of sanctification and
holiness. Special thanks to my mother Merlene Hodge
for being my momma and her unfailing love, hard
work, encouragement and support.

Thanks to Holam books for once again taking another
chance with me, believing and supporting this
project. Additionally, I am appreciative for the editor
and my sister in Christ Cathy Palmer for her time -
and encouraging feedback.

Foreword

God has called this woman of God, a pen as a ready writer. In her book, Get It Before It Gets You, Author Kelly Shaw shares with us, a unique style of teaching biblical truths, from the Word of God, equipping us to obtain deliverance, salvation, and restoration that brings forth freedom and liberty.

Kelly's transparency of her own life experiences and her, as she would say "I just have to keep it real" mentality, allows her to connect with people of all ages. As one of my God-given spiritual daughters, I will never forget sharing with Kelly my testimony and how God delivered me from my own personal **It** in comparison to her **It**.

I believe this volume will yield treasures to those who truly embrace this literary work that will bring about the necessary adjustments to get on the right path and reach your God given destiny.

Truly, Get **It** before **It** Gets You is a life altering book, that will release you into new levels of transparency with God, deliverance from the sin in your life and propel you to freedom and liberty that can be found only in Jesus Christ our Lord. Get **It** Before **It** Gets You is a great investment to sow into the life of your daughter(s), cousin, niece, grand-daughter, sister and friend.

Enjoy the journey,

Anita Dawson
 Overflow Ministries, Inc.
www.overflowministriesinc.org

Preface

It started with the Call.

Have you ever been minding your own business, living your life and bam, out of nowhere, God decides without invitation to interrupt your life? Not long ago, God did just that. I was comfortable in my sin, minding my own business when, out of nowhere, God, without an invite or notice, intruded into my life and told me to stop fornicating (having sex outside of marriage). I was not happy and to be honest, I was bothered by this interruption and I ignored His request.

Most people would say that God is a huge part of their life. I would contend that if we are honest, when it comes to God, some people prefer to call their own shots and expect God to be on board with their decisions. To be honest, I was one who treated God like a Genie in the bottle. I only wanted God to grant my wishes and do what I wanted Him to do. I wasn't interested in anything else. I lived in a constant state of rebellion by not doing what God told me to do. At the time I didn't realize I was disconnected from God because of my sin filled life. Although I rebelled against God, I still wanted to benefit from the blessings of God. I wanted the blessings but I didn't want God to call the shots.

It wasn't long before I suffered the consequences of my disobedience of not doing what God had told me to do. In this rebellious stage of my life, I experienced some dark places and endured some very tough times. When we rebel against God, we are not the only ones who are affected. Ultimately our children become affected.

God was calling me into a life of sanctification (set apart for sacred use) and holiness (complete devotion to God) the problem was......, I was not having it! I liked my sin, I was comfortable in it and I wasn't interested in changing. In March of 2005, I arrived at a crossroad in life, where I had to make a decision. The Lord met me at that crossroad and I made the choice to follow Him. God wants us to serve Him and serve Him only. We are either going to be for Him or against Him. There is no in-between when it comes to God. Our lives should be fashioned around the Word of God and God's Word alone.

"Get It before It Gets You" allows us to identify the It (sin) in our lives and helps us to understand the importance and urgency of getting rid of the It (sin) before It, has the opportunity to destroy us. In the book of *James 1:14-15* we find these words;

But every man is tempted, when he is drawn away of his own lust, and enticed. 15 Then when lust hath conceived, it bringeth forth sin: and sin, when it is finished, bringeth forth death. (KJV)

"Get **It** before **It** Gets You" was birth through my own personal experience of rebellion. My personal **It** (sin) that I refused to deal with was fornication and idolatry. My refusal to obey God didn't bring immediate consequences. I believe God was giving me time to deal with my **It** before **It** ultimately destroyed me. Your **It** might be different from mine, but all **Its** bring about consequences. I penned this book, to share my testimony, so that others will learn from my past mistake and choose not to follow the same path. It is my prayer; with the turn of each page, you will allow the Holy Spirit to help you identify your **It** so you can "Get **It** Before **It** Gets You". It is also my prayer that as you begin to hear God speak, you open up your heart to receive the truth and have the courage and strength to take action.

Thank you for allowing me the opportunity to share with you my struggles that ultimately led to victory. I am confident that if you open up your heart to receive, you too will be victorious over your **It**. – Kelly

Chapter 1 - Under the Influence

Here in the United States, driving under the influence of a controlled substance is against the law. There are many consequences when this law is broken. You could go to jail, lose your driving privilege and in some states, be required to get a special license plate identifying you as a past offender. This law is not set up to be ignored. It is not only set up to protect potential victims, but also set up to protect the perpetrator from getting hurt or killed as well. Being under the influence of any controlled substance can cause a person to become impaired and incompetent. It can also cause someone to lose the ability to function at their full potential which then leads to poor performance.

When I was a child my parents used to always warn me about being around certain crowds of people. They warned me because they didn't want me to be influenced by the wrong people. They didn't want me hanging around people who were having sex, using drugs or getting into trouble. My parents were using their parental instinct to shield me from possible harm. I used to hate when they did this. I didn't see it as a form of protection; I saw it as their way of trying to control my life. In the same way that our parents try to lead us in the right direction, God has given us His Word as instruction to lead and guide us in the right direction but so many times we fail to follow God's direction and end up in trouble. I have to admit like most, I ignored my parents warning and eventually, I found myself under the influence of a teenage boy and a controlled substance, participating in the very things, my parents had warned me about.

The first time I had sex was during my freshman year in high school. Before that, while in middle school and according to the stories that generated from my peers (who keep in mind, were active and well experienced), I had very little knowledge about sex. I often wondered if I was the only one who hadn't had a sexual experience because the people I hung out with were already involved in some type of sexual activity. I often questioned my lack of sexual involvement and wondered if something wrong with me. Sex seemed to come natural to them, and it seemed weird that I was not at all interested.

The summer leading into my freshmen year of high school started off as usual. I was raised on a street called Midland Avenue, in Columbus, Ohio, in the area known as "The Hilltop". Some of my best summers were spent on Midland. The kids in my neighborhood always found something to do and we all stuck together. There was never a dull moment. Quite often, kids from other streets would come over to our street to hang out. Drive by shootings and gang banging were unheard of. Growing up on Midland, the closest you would come to a battle would be a break dancing challenge. I must say, Midland had some of the best break dancers. Every now and then a bike would get stolen or a fight would break out, but by the end of the week everything was back cool again. One thing that is true about the people that grew up on the Hilltop is that we all stuck together.

Even though my summer started as usual, towards the end, there was a slight interruption. I had had boyfriends before and other than hanging out, and every now and then a kiss that was coerced by friends, there was no other type of interaction. I never really liked the idea of French kissing (which in my opinion was basically trading saliva). To get a kiss from me was something huge and terrifying, because I didn't know how to kiss. Although I was forbidden to have a boyfriend, I ignored my parent's rules and began to secretly date this young man my freshman year of high school. I barely made it out of middle school sex free. The challenge I faced was that, I now dated someone who was very experienced in sex. Soon after I began to date him, I have to admit, the relationship scared me because I knew it was only a matter of time before he would want to take the relationship to the next level.

The time finally came and he expressed his strong desire to have sex. He was constantly in my ear about it. I used all kinds of excuses to keep from giving in. I really liked him and I didn't want to lose him, but I knew the only way to continue in the relationship was to give in. I had many fears when it came to sex; none of which were biblically based. I had heard all types of horror stories about the initial first time. Although the stories frightened me, what concerned me the most, was not the possibility of getting a STD (sexually transmitted disease) or getting pregnant, but what worried me the most was, what would happen if I didn't give in. I couldn't stand the thought of being rejected. I continued to dodge the sex conversation, but one day my excuses ran out and I could no longer use the excuse **"I might get pregnant"**, or **"We might get caught".** I found myself in a place where I felt I had no other choice but to lend my body to his sexual desire that led me on an unfamiliar journey down a road called sin.

The day that I had my first sexual experience, I was caught totally off guard. I was not at all prepared mentally or physically to have sex. **I had on smurf underwear that day that read "Have a smurfy day"** and there was nothing smurfy about what was about to go down. There I was, in a smoke filled dark basement with slow music playing in the background and a persistent boyfriend, using well-rehearsed and convincing words, to persuade and assure me, that everything was going to be cool. I was extremely nervous and uneasy but he had a cure for that. He had me smoke some marijuana to help me to relax. Once I reached cloud nine, I found myself having sex while under the influence of a well experienced boy (who was not my husband) and an illegal controlled substance.

In order for us to effectively deal with our **It** (sin), we must first find its root. We need to ask the question "how did this start?" and "how did I get trapped in this?" Often times when we are caught up or trapped in our **It** we are clueless to how we got there in the first place. We need to know where our **It** got started, to better understand how to deal with the **It**.

In the book of Genesis 3:1 a woman named Eve, finds herself under the influence of a serpent that causes her to disobey God.

> *Genesis 3:1-5 Now the serpent was more subtil than any beast of the field which the LORD God had made. And he said unto the woman, Yea, hath God said, Ye shall not eat of every tree of the garden? 2 And the woman said unto the serpent, we may eat of the fruit*

of the trees of the garden: 3 But of the fruit of the tree which is in the midst of the garden, God hath said, Ye shall not eat of it, neither shall ye touch it, lest ye die. 4 And the serpent said unto the woman, Ye shall not surely die: 5 For God doth know that in the day ye eat thereof, then your eyes shall be opened, and ye shall be as gods, knowing good and evil. (KJV)

Eve found herself in a conversation with a serpent. The text suggests that the serpent was challenging and undermining what Eve said God told her, by casting doubt. Here is where Eve messed up. Instead of shutting the serpent down, Eve continued to allow the serpent in her ear and the influences of his conversation led her away from God's will. When God gives us His instruction, we should not welcome any dialog that will deter us from executing God's will in our lives. Eve should have immediately shut the conversation with the serpent down. Many of us have gotten into some bad situation by welcoming and participating in conversations when we should have **KEPT IT MOVING**. To keep it real, most of us are clear on what is required of us to live holy (devoted to God) and sanctified (set apart for God's use) lives, but because we love to entertain ungodly (sinful, wicked) conversation it causes us to fall for the okie doke every time. Some of us have found ourselves in crazy situations that if we would have just shut the conversation down, we wouldn't have to raise kids alone, we wouldn't have caught that STD, been exposed to an abusive man, been turned onto drugs and we would still have money in the bank. If Eve would've shut the conversation down, she would still be chilling in the garden.

As I look back and think about my first sexual encounter, (which later ended in rejection) it wasn't long before I found myself in a repetitive cycle of fornication (having sex outside of marriage), that led to heartbreak after heartbreak that continued through my adult life. Experiencing numerous failed relationships, finally during my early thirties, one particular relationship, led to my breaking point in life. One evening I was at a club minding my own business when Mr. Ugly approached me. Everything in me said he was ugly but here is where things went wrong. I engaged in conversation and a drink with him. I have to admit, his conversation was great and with a little help from some Hypnotic and grapefruit juice (an alcohol beverage), he began to look better. The more I drank, the more he became easy on the eyes and the more he talked, the more I became interested. In a short span of time, while under the influence of conversation and alcohol and against my better judgment, I had somehow convinced myself, that if I dated someone ugly, he would treat me right. To my surprise, out of everybody I dated, he dogged me the worst. What was also different about this time around versus times prior, I had convinced myself that I was not having sex. I was tired of failed relationship, so I decided I was going to hold out until marriage. I didn't take this stand because I was trying to do it the way God required, I was doing it because I was tired of the relationship not lasting.

Over the course of time, his conversation won me over and we began to date. I shared my intentions and he pretended to respect my wishes. We continued to date and sex never came up in our conversations. I really thought that it was working out this time, things were coming along great. I started spending a lot of time at his house, and it quickly went from just visiting to staying overnight, to failing to abstain from sex. The very thing I said I would not do, I found myself right back doing. Once again instead of shutting down the conversation, I took the bait and found myself right back at the door of regret. This experience was so embarrassing that I use to be too ashamed to talk about it. Prior to this relationship, I always dated nice looking men but because all those relationships had failed, I figured that if I dated someone ugly, I would be treated better, but that was not the case, I actually was treated worse. I told myself for the 99th time that this time around would be different (how wrong I was).

Eve allowed the serpent to lure her with the bait conversation that redirected her attention in the direction that was forbidden. Looking at the tree (which was pleasant to her eyes) and now convinced that the tree was good for food, she took of the fruit, and gave also to her husband Adam and they both ate.

> *Genesis 3:6 And when the woman saw that the tree was good for food, and that it was pleasant to the eyes, and a tree to be desired to make one wise, she took of the fruit thereof, and did eat, and gave also unto her husband with her; and he did eat. (KJV)*

The serpent used his mouth piece and persuasion to cause Eve to give in to his influence. Operating under the influence of the serpent did not only cause her to sin, but the text suggests that she convinced Adam to do the same.

I shared earlier that my childhood boyfriend was

experienced in sex. Someone influenced him, he in turn influenced me. In the same way the serpent influenced Eve and Eve influenced Adam and the cycle continues. The enemy's plan to deter us from following God's will and way, does not just involve us. It involves others around us. When we're under an influence, it spills over into the lives of our children, friends and other relationships, causing them to pick up the same patterns of behavior. The serpent initiated his influence on Eve, but the effect of it trickled into Adam's life causing both to sin.

When God gives us His instruction on how we are to live as Christians and we allow someone or something to steer us away from the path we should take, it causes our fellowship to be broken with God. I'm sure most of us can relate to the repercussions that followed after breaking rules our parents had set. If your upbringing was anything like mine, there were consequences for breaking the rules. When I broke the rules, it caused me to be out of fellowship (in good standing) with my parents, I was no longer in their good graces. Broken fellowships often produce shame, anger, embarrassment, resentment and bitterness.

When Adam and Eve allowed the influence of the serpent to take precedence over what God commanded them, it opened the door to sin, which in turn, broke their fellowship with God. When they chose to eat from the forbidden tree, it caused their eyes to become opened only to discover they were naked.

> *Genesis 3:7-10 And the eyes of them both were opened, and they knew that they were naked; and they sewed fig leaves together, and made themselves apron. 8 And they heard the voice of the LORD God walking in the garden in the cool of the day: and Adam and his wife hid themselves from the presence of the LORD God amongst the trees of the garden. 9 And the LORD God called unto Adam, and said unto him, Where art thou? 10 And he said, I heard thy voice in the garden, and I was afraid, because I was naked; and I hid myself. (KJV)*

After eating from the forbidden tree, they discovered they were naked and covered themselves with fig leaves, hiding amongst the trees of the garden. The posture they took to cover and hide, might suggest that they were ashamed and/or afraid. That's normally the result of what happens to us when we break fellowship with God. When God calls us out of a lifestyle of sin, we tend to cover our shame with the fig leaves of alcohol, men or women, drugs (illegal or prescribed), sex, makeup, hair styles, titles, fashion, cigarettes, and other people. God is calling us and because of our sin, we are hiding from the presence of Him. Adam and Eve hid amongst the trees of the garden, which if you think about it, a tree cannot fully hide you; part of you will always be left exposed. I had to ask myself "what were Adam and Eve thinking when they picked that particular hiding spot", but then I thought about us today and how we choose some crazy things to hide behind. Some hide behind excuses, past failures, parents, people, careers, relationships, lies, denial, status, the past, lack of education, and money. When the guilt of broken fellowship is felt, instead of trying to figure out how to get back right, we tend to find places to hide from God. We may even be able to hide from people, but it's impossible to hide from God.

It is not exactly clear why God forbade Adam and Eve from eating from the forbidden tree, but it seems that the restriction was intended for their own good. Growing up there were times when my parents had forbade me from having a boyfriend, or to hang out with a certain crowd or a particular person. They didn't always give me reasons why. Like some, I did not always follow their instruction and as a result I got in trouble and as I continued down that path, I soon found myself pregnant at age sixteen.

We will all encounter situations similar to the Garden of Eden experience, where the enemy will try to lure us with his influential conversation and persuade us to go against God's will and way, but we should learn from Eve's mistake and refuse to participate in conversation with anyone that is speaking contrary to the word of God.

Most of us know what it means to be drunk. I have gotten drunk plenty of times, but while I was drunk I was doing things that I would not have done if I were sober. For some reason, while drunk, I didn't see anything wrong with my ability to function. In my drunkenness, even though my speech was slurred and I staggered when walked, I couldn't see how ridiculous I looked. Being under the influence of alcohol impaired my speech, mobility and my ability to reason. In the same sense when we are under the influence of someone or something, we lose our ability to function properly and our sense of reason goes right out the window and before long, our speech is slurred (making no sense) and we stagger through life looking ridiculous.

In the kingdom of God, the only influence we should be under is the power of the Holy Spirit. The Holy Spirit is given to lead and guide in righteousness and protect us from all other influences. God's Word is so clear that we should not be under the influence of sin. When we allow ourselves to be under the influence of sin, we experience broken fellowship with God and we will always find ourselves covering up with the fig leaves of the world, hiding from the presence of God.

Journal

What are you under the influence of?

What conversations do you need to shut down?

What fig leaves are you covering up with?

What are you hiding amongst?

What is your plan for moving forward?

Chapter 2 - Idol Worship

No one could have told me in a millions years, that I would be guilty of idolatry (idol worship). Primarily because I thought an idol was just a graven image (statue) carved out of wood. Although this is true, idolatry is not limited to just the worship of graven images. Idolatry is worshipping anything other than The One and True Living God. Whatever creature (created being) or things we worship (look upon, give reverent honor, putting confidence and our trust in), becomes an idol and it causes us to become unclean (filthy) and defiled (tainted) in the sight of God. Idol worship is not always easy to detect. Without having the correct and full understanding of what it is, it is easy to slip into it gradually and without notice. I am embarrassed to say that in the past, I participated in idol worship but because of the lack of knowledge, I did not know it at the time.

In the year of 2001, God told me to come out of fornication (having sex with someone I wasn't married to). I was laying right next to my then fiancé. If I remember correctly, it was a Sunday afternoon. God clearly told me to come out of it. I didn't have to guess if it was the Lord speaking, I knew it was God, but I had a better idea. I told God "It's okay Lord, we're getting married." I was crazy enough to try and justify the fact that we were engaged and that His request should not apply to my situation. I'm surprised He didn't strike me down right then. I must pause here and thank Him for His grace and mercy that allowed me the time to get it together. God continued to speak to me about having sex outside of marriage. I remember hearing Him speak and I closed my eyes real tight to get rid of His voice. As He continued to speak to me, I continued to tune Him out. His voice became fainter each time I rejected His request. Looking back, and knowing what I know now, I just can't help but to thank Him for allowing me another chance to get it right.

God's voice faded as time progressed and because nothing bad happened right away, I thought I was home free. When I refused to stop having sex outside of marriage, my disobedience opened the door that lead to idolatry. I felt like I would lose my relationship if I stopped having sex. Instead of honoring God with my obedience, I rejected Him and honored my relationship instead. I placed my relationship above God. Of course, at that time I didn't see it as being idol worship. Things seemed cool for a while; everything seemed to be really coming together. I like to refer to this as **(the calm before the storm).** My fiancé at the time gave me my engagement ring a few days before Christmas and I immediately began making wedding plans. By the beginning of the year, I had set the date, purchased my wedding dress and bridesmaid dresses. In retrospect, red flags were popping up during the planning phase but because I was determined to get married, I ignored them.

I began to notice that my fiancé was not as excited as I thought he should be. To make matters worse, I had a fallen out with one of the bride maids and she no longer wanted to be in the wedding which frustrated me. In my frustration, I began to complain and argue with my fiancé and as a result of the argument; I had thrown my ring and called the wedding off. When I called the wedding off, I really didn't mean it, I was bluffing. The first time I had thrown my ring, I apologized and he gave it back but he told me if I threw it again, I was not getting it back. Of course I didn't take him serious and during another disagreement, I had thrown it again. That time he didn't give it back. Under the impression that he was bluffing, I skeptically continued making wedding plans, despite not having my ring.

On Valentine's weekend I attended my cousin's wedding in Virginia. Prior to leaving, my fiancé bought me a gift and things seem to be finally getting back on the right track. Before I left for the wedding, we had a conversation that left me hopeful that I would get my ring back when I returned. While I was away at the wedding, we stayed in contact and there was no indication of any threat with our relationship. Things seem to be getting better. I was confident that everything was working out. When I returned home from my cousin's wedding, I went from being on top of the world to my world crashing down. I discovered that the man who I had loved for over four years, who I placed all my trust in, had cheated on me while I was away.

I did all I could to resuscitate the relationship. After making multiple attempts of trying to save the relationship, it never fully recovered. I had to finally face the reality, that he no longer wanted to get married and it was time to call the wedding off.
After I called off the wedding, I sank down into a deep depression that lasted a very long time. My life had become a very dark place. I felt like my insides were turned upside down. I tried many things to get rid of the heaviness and despair. The weight of despair was so heavy it began to suffocate me. I felt like I could no longer live or function without him. I had put all my trust and confidence in him and I was willing to do just about anything to have him back. I had placed him above everything and most importantly I placed Him above God. He had become

my idol.

I know many of us have failed to see idol worship in this manner, primarily because many of us have been taught to see idol worship as bowing down and worshipping some type of statue. It was obvious that my relationship took the place of God being Lord over my life. Yes I was going to church and talking about how much I loved the Lord and in my mind I believed it, but my actions communicated the total opposite. When something becomes Lord over our life, it has power and authority over us and becomes our god. The problem with this is, the god we now serve has no power and cannot duplicate The One and True Living God, but the mistake is made in thinking that it can, only to find out that it can't compete. That is why we sometimes find ourselves, frustrated, hurt, betrayed, depressed and going crazy, because the one we placed all our trust and confidence in, has failed. God is the only one who should have that kind of control. We should place our total trust and confidence in Him.

The relationship mattered more than anything to me. I didn't want to come out of the relationship. I didn't like the thought of being alone. I didn't trust that God had my best interest at heart. I wanted to have the say so in whom I wanted to be with. I didn't see anything wrong with what I was doing, to be very honest, I knew that it was not right in God's eyes, but at the time I didn't care. It didn't matter to me what God felt about it, to keep it real, I felt God needed to get with my program because my way was better. During that time in my life, all that mattered was, how I felt and what I wanted.

In this passage of scripture, God spoke these words:

> *Exodus 20:1-5 And God spake all these words, saying, 2 I am the LORD thy God, which have brought thee out of the land of Egypt, out of the house of bondage. 3 Thou shalt have no other gods before me. 4 Thou shalt not make unto thee any graven image, or any likeness of anything that is in heaven above, or that is in the earth beneath, or that is in the water under the earth: 5 Thou shalt not bow down thyself to them, nor serve them: for I the LORD thy God am a jealous God, visiting the iniquity of the fathers upon the children unto the third and fourth generation of them that hate me; (KJV)*

God gave Moses His instruction, on how He wants his people to live. He clearly gives the command that "Thou shalt have no other gods before me. Thou shalt not make unto thee any graven image, or any likeness of anything that is in heaven above, or that is in the earth beneath, or that is in the water under the earth." God continues to provide instruction to not make anything that reflects any type of image that would be used as an instrument to bow down and worship as god. Some would say "That's what they did back in biblical times, nobody does that anymore", or, "that doesn't apply to us now, or that was done back then." We may not be carving images to bow down to, but we do bow down and worship so many things. Bowing is the act of submitting and yielding. It is to bend the head, body, or knee in reverence of something or someone. Some would say that "I don't bow to anything" but I will argue that we may not physically get down on our knees and bow, but our behavior, reflects bowing when we submit and yield, giving reverence to other things and people as (gods).

When we give reverence to God, that He is truly Lord over our lives, it is displayed in our action when we bow submitting and yielding to His will and way. When we **refuse** to bow not submitting and yielding to doing things God way, we place ourselves in the position of bowing to our own agendas, relationships, cars, homes, people, careers and self. As I previously stated, I was willing to do almost anything to hold onto the relationship. My refusal to come out of a fornicated relationship caused me to bow, yield and submit to the relationship rather to the will and way of God. This type of worship was very dangerous to my life and others around me. Not only did it cause me to be frustrated, depressed and stripped of peace, it also caused me to experience God's wrath.

The text in *Exodus 34:14* allows us to see that bowing down and serving anything other than God will provoke Him to jealousy.

> *Exodus 34:14 For thou shalt worship no other god: for the LORD, whose name is Jealous, is a jealous God. (KJV)*

One of God's many attributes is that, He is jealous. I know we have a want to embrace only God's loving side, but let me testify, He also has a jealous side. Many others, me included, have experienced it. When I think of jealous, my mind causes me to understand the correlation of a relationship between a husband and wife. Neither participant in the relationship desires anything that could pose a threat, causing the relationship to be jeopardized. When coming together in the covenant of marriage, both parties promise to be submitted and committed. It is very important not to solicit the input of outside influences (other people) that could pose a threat to the marriage. Just like marital covenants in the physical, God expects us as Christians to be in a covenant relationship with Him, submitted and committed without the threat of outside influences (sin), to jeopardize the covenant we have with Him.

Although we have the proclivity to cling to God's loving side, we still must recognize He has a jealous side, which if triggered, could cause His wrath to be unleashed. In all of my 41 years I have never witnessed jealousy as anything pleasurable. Whether in reality, or in a lifetime movie, jealousy has always had an unpleasant outcome. Some make the comparison and use it to measure how much a person loves them. I am one who has been guilty of this distorted thought process. Let's talk about that for a while. I will be the first to admit that in the past, I measured a man's love by how jealous or crazy he acted towards me and others. I know it sounds crazy for some, but it has, or currently is, reality for others. In retrospect it was crazy, but I'm just keepin- it-real! Yes, I measured love by how jealous they were and as a side note, I purposely did things to make them jealous just to get a certain response and if most are honest, you have too. But since I'm the one writing it's my duty to put it out there. I don't know why we love for others to be a little jealous or a lot jealous. Some would say, "It's flattering" others may say, "It's cute." Most would be frightened, if it began to take on the character trait of a psycho. But all jokes aside, jealousy over time escalates and breeds hostility. Have you watched the news lately? Hostility in most cases if left unchecked could lead to psychotic behavior. As a side note (most of us, at some point in life, have been referred to as psycho). I know we don't like it, but it is what it is.

God wants us to worship and bow to Him only and when we dabble in the worshiping of other people and things it causes Him to become jealous and His jealousy unleashes His wrath. God has strictly said in His Word to have **No** other gods before Him. *"Thou shalt have no other gods before me". (Exodus 20:3)* I with my bold behind, made a choice to disobey God. I didn't carve my idol out of wood or fashioned it out of gold. My idol was a man, a living being (flesh and blood). I worshiped my relationship. I did the very thing that provoked God too jealously and boy if I only knew that I would soon suffer the consequences of my disobedience.

The effects of jealousy, reminds me of the time when I was married to my now ex-husband. During the course of our marriage, he found out that I had been cheating. Prior to me arriving home, I had no idea that he had found out. I arrived at the door and without warning; he confronted me with the evidence. Can you imagine how things went down? I didn't have time to get my lie straight or get my composure together. I'll spare you all the details, but just take a second and try to imagine how he felt and what he wanted to do to me. He didn't embrace me with a "Hi, Dear" or "Hey, Babe," no, his wrath was unleashed. Oh, I forgot to mention, prior to getting caught, I was warned by others of what would happen if I got caught. People were afraid for me. I remember a conversation between me and my friend. She said this to me, "You better stop because if he finds out, he's going to kill you". I blew her comment off, because, I didn't think I would ever get caught. Not believing that I would get caught, led me to believe there would be no consequences. That's the same way we deal with God, just because He hasn't dealt with our sin instantly, we think we will never get caught or suffer the consequences. God is jealous because He loves us and wants all of us. He is not interested in part, He wants it all.

Journal

Identify your idol?

What are you doing to provoke God's wrath?

What steps are you taking to get back in the right relationship with God?

Chapter 3 - The Indictment

Even though the evidence of my sins was mounting against me, it was business as usual for me. I continued in my sin, without any regard to its consequence.

In the judicial system, to be formally charged with a crime, a written statement, charging a party with the commission of a crime is drawn up by the prosecuting attorney. It is then presented to the grand jury to determine if there is probable cause for the arrest of the suspect in custody. During this process, a written statement is prepared of the place, manner and time in which the defendant is alleged to have committed the offence. If probable cause is found, then the defendant will be bound over for trial.

In the book of Ezekiel chapter 23, God is speaking to the prophet Ezekiel concerning two sisters who had committed whoredoms (idolatry). He begins by laying out an indictment against two nations using the parable of two sisters.

Ezekiel 23:1-4 The word of the LORD came again unto me, saying, 2 Son of man, there were two women, the daughters of one mother: 3 And they committed whoredoms in Egypt;

they committed whoredoms in their youth:
there were their breasts pressed, and there they
bruised the teats of their virginity. 4 And the
names of them were Aholah the elder and
Aholibah her sister: and they were mine, and
they bare sons and daughters. Thus were their
names; Samaria is Aholah, and Jerusalem
Aholibah. (KJV)

As Ezekiel sets in motion the indictment, he
starts by disclosing who these two sisters are and
the history and root of where the accusations
originate from. He first describes the older sister
Aholah, whose name in the Hebrew means (her
own tent), represents Samaria (another name for
Israel) and the younger sister Aholibah, whose
name in the Hebrew means (my tent in her)
represents Jerusalem (known also as Judah). By
birth, they were one nation (Israel), until the
splitting of the nation (becoming Samaria and
Jerusalem) after the death of King Solomon, King
David's son, who succeeded him after his death.
The charges brought against these two sisters, is
whoredom (idolatry), a behavior which God states
was learned early in their youth (early
development) in the land of Egypt.

In the book of Exodus, it lays out the foundation,
of the early development of the once united nation.

The Israelites were oppressed and treated very poorly in their early stages of development, while enslaved in Egypt. The prophet Ezekiel compares the under developed nation to a young, innocent, under developed girl, who had been mishandled and mistreated. By using the illustration of a young, innocent, under developed girl, Ezekiel communicates to us, how Israel, in its delicate nature, was mistreated and mishandled in the land of Egypt, in the same way we would see how a young, naive girl, left to herself, would fall victim in the same sense.

When the Israelites, (once known as the Hebrews) first came to Egypt, they were small in number and had not yet developed into a nation. While enslaved in Egypt, the Lord increased them tremendously over a period of 430 years, developing them into a nation that would later become the nation of Israel. The text also allows us to see, that their whorish behavior started early in their youth (in the early stages of their development) in Egypt. It is believed that it was in Egypt that they were exposed to and picked up whorish ungodly behaviors. (*Ezekiel 23:3*)

Most of us can relate to being exposed, oppressed and mistreated in our own personal Egypt (place of bondage), in the early stages of life, enslaved under the rule of satan (our modern day Pharaoh). It was there, in our bondage, where we picked up the habit of ungodliness, defiling (to make dirty, polluting) ourselves with the idol of sin. God delivered the Hebrew people from Egypt. The Israelites had been in bondage for 430 years. During that time, they were exposed to the Egyptian routine and way. It wasn't enough for God to just deliver them from Egypt, although they moved physically to another location, they still carried with them, the habits and practices of Egyptian influence. God had to teach them how to be His people. He did this by giving them His law. *(Exodus 24:12)* There was a lot to learn and old habits to break (Egyptian habits). God told Moses (the one God chose to lead the people out of Egypt), to come up into Mount Sinai, so He could give him the law and commandments to teach the people. Moses left his brother Aaron and Hur in charge while he went up to Mount Sinai to receive the commandments. *(Exodus 24:12-14)* While Moses was up on Mount Sinai and because of the length of time that had lapsed, the people requested that Aaron make a god that they could worship. Aaron honored their request by making a molten calf. *(Exodus 32: 1-4)*

It has been specifically stated in other text, that they yielded to idol worship in Egypt, while in bondage.

(Joshua 24:14, Ezekiel 20:8, Ezekiel 23:3-8) It is likely, that the people's request of Aaron to produce a god, originated from Egypt where they had recently lived and participated in Egyptian idol worship. Moses gave the children of Israel God's law and commandments concerning the crafting, possession and worship of other gods. God specifically told them not to make, keep or worship other gods. *Exodus 20:3-5*

When we function under the influence of sin and continue to ignore God's commands and laws, we will find ourselves in the same predicament as these two sisters, indicted. As we continue to look at the text, the prophet continues to allow us to see that it was in Egypt, that they suffered abuse. God continues to lay out the indictment, now focusing on Aholah (Samaria another name for Israel). He shares that Aholah played the harlot, by lusting after the Assyrians. These were men who were of high status, held titles and were very desirable. She committed these ungodly acts, and defiled herself with them. God is charging Aholah with harlotry. He first states that Aholah belonged to Him.

> *Ezekiel 23:5 And Aholah played the harlot when she was mine; and she doted on her lovers, on the Assyrians her neighbours, 6 Which were clothed with blue, captains and*

rulers, all of them desirable young men, horsemen riding upon horses. 7 Thus she committed her whoredoms with them, with all them that were the chosen men of Assyria, and with all on whom she doted: with all their idols she defiled herself. (KJV)

A harlot (whore), according to how it is defined, is a woman who engages in unlawful sexual intercourse, in sexual acts for money (prostitution) and who is sexually promiscuous. According to the word of God, sex is unlawful when committed outside of marriage. So the moment a woman exposes her body to someone other than her spouse for sexual purpose, if single, she's guilty of **fornication**, if married, she is guilty of **fornication** and **adultery**, once the act is committed. As I was growing up, I never really heard people use the word whore a lot. It was not a term that was frequently used in my home or community. The word we used to describe whorish behavior was the term "hoe". Although Webster defines hoe as a gardening tool, where I come from it is often used to portray whorish behavior, but with an extended description. While doing research for this book, I polled some people and asked them to define the term hoe. What hit the top of the list was, promiscuous, nasty, unrestrained, loose, having multiple partners and prostitution. A condensed interpretation would be someone who sleeps around.

The point is, the word "hoe", never yielded anything positive. Surprisingly many of us have or currently are, involved in promiscuous sexual activity. I did a small survey with a group of women, asking how they viewed promiscuity. Here are some of their thoughts: horny, whorish, free with self, carefree, sleeping around, dirty, and freaky.

I'm sure some may be wiping their forehead as a sigh of relief saying, "That's not me, because I don't have a lot of partners". Some like to think, that promiscuity is having multiple sex partners in a short time frame or having multiple partners all at the same time. Promiscuity is not measured by the lapse of time between partners, nor the lack in the number of partners. Most of us, if we are really honest and do some self-examinations, most, if not all, have had or are currently indulging in promiscuous behavior, which I hate to say, goes hand and hand with **(okay brace yourself, ladies)** whorish behavior. **(Whew, take a deep breath and exhale slowly.)** I know half of y'all have fainted by now. You're probably asking yourself "Did she just say whorish???" **(I did)**, now let's move on.

I'm sure no one, wants their sexual experience to be compared to whorish conduct, I'm with you on that and I know it's a hard pill to swallow, but some of us if honest, have made a hoe move (committed a whorish act) at some point. I'm convinced that there are three types of promiscuous women. There are the bold ones, who do their dirt all out in the open, who could care less what anybody thinks. There are the closet ones, who are more discrete, keeping theirs on the down low, not wanting anyone to know the truth. Last, but not least, the ones who desperately want to be loved, who sleep around, hoping to receive love in exchange. Whether done discretely or indiscreetly, promiscuous is still promiscuous. You might say "I only had sex with one person", although that's not considered promiscuous, it still falls under the umbrella of fornication, which is to engage in sex outside of marriage, which is not the way God intends for sex to be utilized. Some may try to use the excuse that they have been together for ump-teen years and are considered "common-law married". Let me help you, living together does not qualify you as married. I have heard different explanations used to justify fornication. Here are some of the explanations given:

- **Each time I had sex, I was in a relationship**
- **I consider myself common law married.**
- **I didn't sleep with just anybody. I'm very picky**
- **I lived with the person I slept with**
- **I'm having sex with the man I will soon marry**

- **God made sex for us to enjoy.**
- **I'm cool, I use protection.**
- **I haven't had that many partners**
- **I am not screwing everybody just my kid's daddy**

These are only a few of the many excuses, used to justify fornication. **Let's keep it real, girlfriend, you can't justify wrong, it is, what it is!**

We touched on idol worship and God's displeasure of it in the previous chapter. As I shared before, my refusal to come out of fornication, led me into idolatry. Idolatry and fornication go hand in hand. They are thick as thieves; where you find one, you can best believe the other is close by. Disobeying God's command to stop fornicating, led me into idolatry. Do you see the connection? Disobedience of one thing (fornication) led to another thing (idol worship). God delivered Israel out of the land of Egypt and He made a covenant with them. (*Exodus 19:5*) He also commanded Israel not to have any dealings with surrounding nations because of the risk of becoming involved in idol worship. The surrounding nations' influence would be a snare to them. (*Exodus 23:31-33, Exodus 34:11*)

Israel was in a covenant relationship with God. In order for the covenant not to become violated,

Israel had to obey God's voice and keep His commands. The same is true for us, that in order for us to continue to be in a covenant relationship with God we must obey God's voice and keep his commands. Aholah was in a covenant relationship with God, but it didn't stop her from doting on (lusting after) the Assyrians her neighbors. The Assyrians are described as men of high rank, young and desirable. Aholah (Israel) admired the Assyrians military strength and power and placed her trust in them. *(2 Kings 15:19, 20 & 2 Kings 17:3)*

As Christians, even though we live in the world, we should not become like the world. *(Romans 12:2)* God wants us to trust Him and to look to Him for our daily provisions and protection. Aholah admired and sought the protection of the Assyrians, which brought God displeasure. How often do we bring God displeasure as a result of our sin? It is when we take our eyes off God and begin to dote (look) upon others and desire things that are not pleasing to God. We have to be careful with who and what we link up with and who and what we put our trust in, because it could lead to other things. Yes, the Assyrians looked good, they were young, high in rank and strong, but God commanded Israel not to link up with surrounding nations because it would lead them into worshipping idols.

After Aholah hooked up with (made an alliance) with Assyria, it wasn't long before she began to worship their idols

> *Ezekiel 23:7 Thus she committed her whoredoms with them, with all them that were the chosen men of Assyria, and with all on whom she doted: with all their idols she defiled herself. (KJV)*

Israel became defiled after hooking up with Assyria. They committed Spiritual Fornication by worshipping the Assyrians idols. God had warned Israel in Exodus 34:11-16 not to make any covenants with other nations, because it would cause them to worship other gods. The very thing that God warned them against was the very thing they did. Most of us can identify with Aholah, where we have joined up with someone or something that God does not approve of. Yes we liked what we saw and went after it. If we can be honest some of us knew that God would not be pleased but because of our strong desire, we were willing to take the chance. In 2 Corinthians 6:14, Paul shares with us the importance of not being unequally yoked (tied) with unbelievers.

> *2 Corinthians 6:14 Be ye not unequally yoked together with unbelievers: for what fellowship hath righteousness with*

unrighteousness? And what communion hath light with darkness? (KJV)

Paul goes on to ask the question, "What fellowship hath righteousness with the unrighteousness?" and "what communion hath light with darkness. I would suggest that Paul (in the same sense that God warned Israel in Exodus 34:11-16), warns us today the importance of not being yoked to unbelievers. We can believe that Paul's warning is intended to help us understand and to prevent us from worshipping and engaging in someone or something that is not pleasing to God and that is exactly what we do, when we become involved with things that God does not approve of.

When Aholah joined up with the Assyrians she also defiled (made unclean) her self by worshipping their idols. So often we as (Christians), convince ourselves into thinking that we can dabble in ungodliness, but not get caught up. Many of us hook up with unbelievers and fool ourselves into believing the relationship is right and will last and find ourselves doing any and everything to get it to work.

The Assyrians were an elite group of men who held high positions. Some women will sell themselves out for a man of elite status, wealth, a high position or good looks. Today we have many examples of women, who go after men with money or status, thinking "This is the life!" but the reality is, it wasn't what they bargained for. They believed wealth and status was enough to sustain them, only to find themselves in the middle of a scandal or divorce. Others have placed their trust in good looks or how great the sex was, only to find out, that was all it was to them and that they were not the only one. We have to be careful where, who and what we put our trust in. The very thing you put your trust in, could one day be the very thing you will soon regret.

God continues to lay out the indictment, sharing how Aholah continued to operate in ungodly behavior that she brought from Egypt.

> *Ezekiel 23:8 Neither left she her whoredoms brought from Egypt: for in her youth they lay with her, and they bruised the breasts of her virginity, and poured their whoredom upon her. (KJV)*

The text suggests that it's possible to carry old habits and behaviors learned early in life, with us, into new places. Most would think that once God delivered her (Israel) out of the land of Egypt, she (Israel) would no longer be interested in that type of lifestyle. Although Aholah had left the place of bondage, she still carried the residue of Egyptian behavior. We can clearly see that Aholah was mishandled early in her life (her innocence was violated). Does this sound familiar? Some of us by no fault of our own have been violated or taken advantage of early in life. Just as Aholah, there are those who have been mishandled sexually by someone who stole their virginity under the false pretense of "I love you", or your innocence was violated by a father, relative, babysitter or a complete stranger, who wouldn't take no for an answer. There are so many ways to be mishandled. It could be abandonment, false accusations, violation of trust and being lied to.

Deliverance of the offense may have taken place for some, where you are no longer exposed to the violator but, like Aholah, you are now a carrier of the residue of the violation. You're probably asking "what does she mean by carrier of the residue?" Residue is the remainder of something, the left over. When we are violated, it is possible to be delivered from the hands of the person that committed the violation, but still be a carrier of the residue of the violation. Okay let me break it down. If a person has been molested, hurt, rejected, misled, or abandoned by someone and that someone has been sent to jail, died or is no longer around, the person who was violated, has been delivered from the violator, but may still carry the scars, (residue) of the violation.

It has been said that some people who have been a victim, being exposed to certain behaviors, end up repeating those same cycles. This has been verified in a judicial setting as a result of an investigation into a person's background. Before a person convicted of a crime is sentenced, the court system does what is called a PSI (pre-sentence investigation). This report is used to help the courts determine the appropriate sentence. Some of the information includes family history, education, health, arrest record, substance abuse and mental health issues. This is an investigation of the person's history to determine if there are special circumstances that would warrant a lighter sentence or a history of a criminal behavior that would increase the harshness of the sentence. During these investigations, in some cases it has been found that the accused was once a victim themselves of either the same accusation or something similar.

I'm sure, like Aholah, we all have had our own Egypt experience, where we were victimized and introduced and operated in corrupt behaviors. We've been delivered from the place of bondage but still carry the scars (residue) of the experience.

Journal

How many of us can identify with Aholah?

What have we carried around or refuse to let go of or continue to indulge in, that continues to displease God?

Does God have an indictment against you?

Chapter 4 - Blind Spot

Have you ever been driving, went to get over, and almost had an accident because you didn't see the car in the next lane because it was in your blind spot. A blind spot is an area of the road that cannot be seen while looking forward or through the rear view or side mirrors. Vehicles that are in adjacent lanes of the road, that fall into these blind spots may not be visible using the car's mirrors. This area of road can be viewed only by a brief turn of the head or by installing mirrors with larger fields of view. Not taking the necessary steps to check your blind spot, could put you at risk for a possible accident.

I'm sure when Aholah first hooked up with the Assyrians, she never thought things would take a turn for the worst. Aholah was so blinded by what she wanted that going into it, she never saw the trouble that was coming.

God shares that because Aholah loved, trusted and lusted after the Assyrians He turned her over to the Assyrians.

Ezekiel 23:9 Wherefore I have delivered her into the hand of her lovers, into the hand of the Assyrians, upon whom she doted. (KJV)

Once God handed her over, it wasn't long before the Assyrians, (the very ones she hooked up with and placed all her trust in) spied her out and discovered her blind side, attacking her, stripping (exposing her nakedness) her of all her beauty and protection, carrying her children into captivity, destroying her and her future. As a result of this, she suffered shame and embarrassment because all her business was now out in the open and she was "put on blast."

Ezekiel 23:10 These discovered her nakedness: they took her sons and her daughters, and slew her with the sword: and she became famous among women; for they had executed judgment upon her. (KJV)

Quite a few of us can relate to Aholah in the same sense, where we link up with someone or something that was not blessed by God and refuse to come out of it. We knew what was required of us but suppressed God's truth (held the truth hostage in our unrighteousness) and continued in our wrong doing. Regardless of the previous warnings and what the Word of God said, it didn't matter, we were still bent on getting what we wanted. We continued to move forward in the direction that we knew wasn't pleasing to God and found ourselves given over to a reprobate mind (foolish and bull headed, determined to remain in a state of mind that is opposed to God's will and way). In other words, to keep it real, this is how it goes down. When we are hell bent on doing things the way we want and are not interested in correction and continue to omit what is right, (especially having the knowledge of God's truth), God steps back and says "okay" and leaves us alone and allows us to continue to do what we do, which will eventually cause us to look dumb and stupid, because somewhere in our mind, we have conjured up a lie and changed who God is, by rejecting His will and way by establishing our own rules, by creating and worshipping our own type of gods (idols). We fool ourselves into believing the god we created would be a better fit for our lives. *(Romans 1:21-25)*

This is done so much, that I don't think we really understand the dangers of it. It's never a good thing to go against God's will and way. I'm sure many of us can testify that the outcome of going against the will and way of God has led them down a path of destruction. I am a living witness and here to tell you that I lost a lot of things and went through a very dark and depressing time where I almost lost my mind, while traveling that path. There are some of you reading this right now, who clearly knows you are doing things that are not pleasing to God. You have been consumed and caught up in this cycle for so long that you have become blinded by your own delusion that you no longer can determine the difference between reality and fantasy. You have convinced yourself and are trying to convince others by making excuses for the mess, only to sound and look ridiculous. Everyone else around you knows the truth, but you don't seem to get it. Because you've been at this for such a long time and your refusal to embrace God's will and way, it has caused God to release you, letting you do your thing, which leads down the path of destruction. *(Romans 1:32)* Some people can't tolerate God's will and way, so they seek to exchange it for a lie, in order to accommodate their wants and desires.

News about Israel's (Aholah) destruction and what had happen to her traveled quickly. All her business was out. It was no secret why she ended up in the condition that she did. Her ruin became an object of conversation. Aholah was amazed by the Assyrians lavishness and power which caused her to desire and seek their protection instead of seeking God. Not long after hooking up with the Assyrians, did Aholah go astray and participated in their worship practices (idol worship). The text allows us to see that this behavior, caused God to hand Aholah over to the very ones (Assyrians), that she desired and placed her trust in. It wasn't long before the Assyrians overpowered Israel (Aholah) destroying her, her children and her future. Aholah didn't value God or His instruction. Like most of us, she thought hers was better. This mind set is dangerous and we can clearly see that when we swap the worship of God the Creator (going against His order and design) for something else, it causes us not to value and honor God. We give a lot of lip service, expressing how we love, and honor and respect God, but our action is what really counts. God handing us over does not have to be permanent, hopefully the experience will cause us to repent and correct the behavior. Repentance must be sought to avoid destruction.

Once God withdrew His protection from Aholah, the Assyrians discovered she no longer had covering (protection). The Assyrians took her children and slew her with the sword. The very ones who Aholah lusted after and made alliance with, were the very ones who God used to execute judgment upon her. The very thing that we do that goes against God, is the very thing He will use as a tool for correction. Sound familiar? I know for myself I have had plenty of embarrassing moments when I disobeyed God by seeking after ungodly relationships. I know firsthand what it's like to disobey God and be left naked in a state of shame for the entire world to see. I wasn't concerned about God's wrath when I was disobeying. I was only interested in the relationship. I placed all my trust in the man and not in God. It's a dangerous thing to disobey God. I can't stress that enough. You may be currently in an ungodly relationship and things may seem good right now, I'm sure while Aholah was involved with the Assyrians it was all good at first. Things always appear to be good in the beginning. You may be thinking that the relationship is perfect but I'm here to tell you that sin has a cost *(Romans 6:23)* and eventually it will be time to pay up.

A lot of times we don't consider how others are affected by the decisions we make. Aholah's children were carried away by the Assyrians. In our own lives, decisions we make, directly affect those connected to us. We don't like to look at it that way, but it's true. Those who are connected to us, especially our children are greatly affected by the decisions we make. Think about it, what decisions have you made that now affect your children? I know for myself, my children watched me go through plenty of ungodly relationships and now they are repeating the same behavior.

I was raised and maybe many of you were raised in the "Do as I say not as I do" setting. I remember my father repeatedly saying this to me and my siblings. Eventually those words became part of my vocabulary with my own children. I watched my dad do a lot of things that he forbade me to do. At the time it seemed harmless, but as I grew older, I believe his sinful behavior influenced my life and began to manifest itself in many different ways. I began to repeat the behaviors I witnessed early in my childhood and it became an open door for the enemy to carry me away from God's intended path.

I was an Aholah at one time and I know what it feels like to be involved in an ungodly relationship. Just like Aholah, it cost me a lot. Like I stated previously, my world came crashing down, and there I was left uncovered and ashamed. I remember that evening when I returned from my cousin's wedding so clearly. After learning that my the finance' had cheated, I found myself on the floor of my room crying so hysterically, that it caused my 16 year old daughter to come in and comfort me, her mother. (Now what's wrong with that picture?) She's the 16 year old daughter, I'm the 30 something year old mother. It should have been the other way around. I should have been the one comforting her after a high school heart break, but noooooooo; there I was a pitiful mess, on the floor crying to her. What a shame!!! I have to go here, we as women wonder what's wrong with our kids when they get to acting crazy. Oh how we get amnesia and forget how we performed and lived crazy in front of them. We need to stay in our role and be the mothers God has called us to be. We are so busy being selfish trying to do our own thing and as a result our kids suffer! It is so true we are some selfish beings that we don't even take the time to count the cost of how our actions affect our kids. I'm the first to admit I'm guilty. My disobedience to God caused me over time to become blind to the point that I could no longer see or discern what was transpiring in my life because of my sin. God was unfolding His wrath in my Blind Spot.

Getting hit in my blind spot caused me a lot of heartache. The relationship quickly deteriorated and by no choice of my own, I had to call the wedding off. That was the most embarrassing moment in my life. I don't know what bothered me the most, calling the wedding off or the questions that followed that filled me with dread. I was sort of cool with dealing with the break up, not that it felt good but at least I could deal with that privately. But calling the wedding off became public information. I was used to masking my true emotions around other people, but how could I mask the wedding being called off. The news of it was sure to travel. This was breaking news that was hot off the press. We love gossip and love to spread it, as long as it doesn't involve us. I was so gripped with fear and concerned about what other people would say and think about me that just the thought of it made me sick at the stomach. This was not supposed to happen to me. I had a reputation to uphold. I didn't want others to see my weakness. I was one that always held it together. I always kept my appearance together. On the outside, I was straight. That's who you saw hidden behind the mask. But now I was faced with my biggest fear, wondering to myself - what are people going to say, how will I respond, and what can I say that will keep me from being embarrassed?

I went over and over in my head how I would respond to the many questions that would be asked. I thought about hiding out, but then thought people would know and talk about that. Then I thought about responding in the "I don't give a %@#!" kind of way, but then I thought people would say I was bitter. I was so consumed in what others would say or think, that fear was constantly taunting me every moment of the day. I dreaded going anywhere because I feared being asked "How's the wedding plans coming", just to say I'm not getting married and then the dreadful question that follows "Why not?" How in the heck was I supposed to explain "why not?" without feeling embarrassed? And the next thing I thought was "why God are you allowing this to happen to me?" Feelings of fear, anger, frustration, grief, bitterness and sadness were all mixing together inside me and I didn't know up from down. I felt very weird. I was not myself. Depression had started to take root and I didn't realize it. It didn't dawn on me that this was resulting from my rebellion. I blamed what I was feeling on everyone and everything but my rebellion. When we operate in disobedience we cause ourselves to be in a state of rebellion. When we rebel against God, it is first His nature to warn us to repent and turn back to Him, but when we continue to ignore His many warnings, (just like I did when He was calling me out of fornication) that is when His wrath is released. God in His Grace and Mercy gives us time to repent and turn to Him. God speaks to the prophet Ezekiel concerning the house of Israel, calling them to repentance and warning them to turn way from their transgressions (**to violate a command or law**) which eventually caused their ruin. *(Ezekiel 18:30)*

Please hear me, **I KNOW FIRST HAND WHAT GOD'S WRATH FEELS LIKE**! I was one that had to see it before I believed it. My momma always told me "A hard head makes a soft behind."

Journal

Who or what are you seeking after that is not pleasing to God?

Are you holding God's truth hostage in your situation?

Do you really know the difference between reality and fantasy?

Are you blinded by what you want so bad that you can't see the warning sign flashing all around you?

Do you easily get upset when others try to tell you the truth?

Do you recognize the danger of going against God's will and way?

Chapter 5 - Pushing the Envelope with Eyes Wide Shut

Not sure if any of you are familiar with the term "pushing the envelope." This is a term used to describe someone's action that goes beyond the limit. If I was to use slang, I would say "You done gone too far." How many of us can admit that at some point in life, we have gone too far and as a result, experienced the wrath of our parents, teacher or someone else. If I was to recite the words my momma used after me or my brother had "pushed the envelope" it would be, "Wait till your daddy gets home." We quickly knew what that meant, we were in big trouble. Even when dealing with my own kids I used similar language like "Keep it up, lightening bout to strike." Not sure what saying you heard or used, but we all can agree that "pushing the envelope" did not usually yield a positive response. As this chapter continues, we will see that Aholah's sister Aholibah, saw firsthand, Aholah's destruction, as a result of disobedience. It will also show how I, continued to push the envelope regardless of my life falling apart.

You would think by now after "getting hit in my blind spot", I would have learned my lesson at this point; seeing how God had dealt with me, in that situation, but oh no, not hard headed Kelly.

Destruction was all around me and even though I could see with my physical eyes my life falling apart, I didn't recognize that it was the result of my disobedience and rebellion. I could see things falling apart but instead of seeing it for what it really was, I didn't make the connection. I was only seeing it from my perspective and made it out to be what I wanted it to be. I saw it as me being wronged by other people. What do I mean by this? Glad you asked. Let's dissect this madness. When things didn't work out in my relationships, job, finances or with my kids, I would blame others. Isn't it funny how when things aren't going right in our lives we tend to blame other people? I was always passing blame onto others and never seeing it for what it really was. As I continued down this destructive path of sin, somewhere in my mind, I believed that I was still in control and like a fool; I was back at it again refusing to stop having sex outside of marriage. Yes I had seen what happened before, but hadn't learned my lesson. I just knew this time around, my way would work. I had it all figured out and didn't feel I needed any assistance from God. I did not want God to control all of my life. I did not invite Him nor was He welcome. I was willing to allow God to control only certain areas of my life but certainly not my relationships and sex life.

The text moves forward with God, directing our

attention to Aholah's sister Aholibah. God shares that when Aholibah (Jerusalem), saw what had happened to her sister Aholah (Israel), it didn't stop her from traveling down that same path. Instead of depending on God's power and protection, she being just like her sister, sought after and trusted in Assyria's power and protection. (*2 Kings 16:7, 8 & 2 Chronicles 28:16*)

Ezekiel 23: 11-13 And when her sister Aholibah saw this, she was more corrupt in her inordinate love than she and in her whoredoms more than her sister in her whoredoms. 12 She doted upon the Assyrians her neighbours, captains and rulers clothed most gorgeously, horsemen riding upon horses, all of them desirable young men.13 Then I saw that she was defiled, that they took both one way. (KJV)

Aholibah saw what happened to her sister, but it didn't seem to stop her from going down the same path. She repeated the same deeds, by employing the Assyrians to protect her that also led to engaging in their idol worship. She not only engaged in idol worship, she made a replica (copy) of an altar she saw in Damascus and had it brought and placed in the temple of the One and True Living God. It doesn't stop there, get this, she even removed the original altar (The brazen altar where sacrifices were offered) from its place and discontinued its purpose by transferring its function onto the new altar (used for idol worship), that was built. Wow isn't that something? Not only was the location of the altar (original place of worship) moved, but it was changed from what God originally intended (2 Kings 16). This still happens today; God expects us to worship Him and to sacrifice our will and way at His altar by following the pattern and order that is found in His Word. Yet some have chosen to remove His altar and replaced it with the altar of their will and way.

I had my own idea of how to worship God. I tried to mix God's will and way with my will and way. I had what is often referred to as, one foot in the church and one foot in the world. I was trying to combine the two. I knew what God's Word said and part of His Word I obeyed while the other parts I ignored. I created my own type of worship. I wanted God's blessings and still wanted to do my own thing. I worshipped at the altar of my will and way and pushed the altar of God (His will and way) to the side. Aholibah, removed and changed the order and way of the brazen altar. She also dismissed its original function, by changing its original purpose. The brazen altar was no longer used to offer sacrifices but would be used to make inquiries of God when needed. (2 *Kings 16)*

For some it's not surprising that God is often pushed aside and only called upon when needed. That has been the story of most of our lives if not currently, definitely at some point in time. For a long time, this was the story of my life. I did not allow God to occupy or function in my life the way that He intended. Although I wanted God in my life, I only wanted Him in the way that I wanted Him to be. I didn't want to fully follow His will and way. I just wanted Him around to request things of Him. I wanted His blessing and that's it.

I can definitely relate to both sisters. Why oh why, do we believe that fat meat ain't greasy, or that if we play with fire we won't get burned? Why do we continue to do things over and over, but swear we will get a different outcome? I have heard it said that "insanity is doing the same thing over and over, expecting a different result." So when we keep doing the same things, expecting different results, what does that say about us? Doesn't that make us a little looney? (Take a moment to ponder that thought).

It wasn't enough for Aholibah to witness the fate of her sister; she continued to push the envelope even more by lusting after images of Chaldean. The prophet Ezekiel goes on to tell us that Aholibah, increased her whordoms, lusting after images of

Chaldean men she saw portrayed on a wall. Not only did Aholibah follow the same path as her sister, she was even more corrupt. Check this out, even after she hooked up with the Assyrians, she still wasn't satisfied; she kicked it up a notch by including Babylonia. *(Ezekiel 16:28 & 2 Kings 12-15)*

Ezekiel 23: 14-16 And that she increased her whoredoms: for when she saw men pourtrayed upon the wall, the images of the Chaldeans pourtrayed with vermilion, 15 Girded with girdles upon their loins, exceeding in dyed attire upon their heads, all of them princes to look to, after the manner of the Babylonians of Chaldea, the land of their nativity: 16 And as soon as she saw them with her eyes, she doted upon them, and sent messengers unto them into Chaldea. (KJV)

The text allows us to understand that Aholibah, lusted after what she saw and then took action by sending for the Babylonians. Let's park here for a moment. A lot of times we have gotten caught up in stuff that we ourselves initiated. We knew better but still insisted on satisfying our flesh. This reminds me of how I continued to seek after the relationship even though it continued to fall apart. It wasn't always that the man who came looking for me, oh no, most of the time I sought after him. With my eyes wide shut,

I continued to try and resuscitate the relationship. The more I tried the more it failed. I didn't recognize that no matter how much I tried it was not going to work. God was not allowing the relationship to work. I believe when God tell us to do something He gives us time to do it but when we refuse, He steps in and take action. God told me to come out of a relationship where I was having sex outside of marriage. He gave me time to do it, but I refused. My disobedience caused God to take action against the relationship. Each time I got back with him, the break up became more intense and I sank deeper and deeper into depression. I even had the nerve to get upset with him, when things fell apart, when in actuality, I should have been upset with myself because I was the one who sent for him. Looking back, I believe I would have been saved a lot of pain and embarrassment, if I would have initially done what God told me versus God having to step in and strip me of it.

The suffering of what I thought was depression, caused me to eventually seek out medical help. I tried counseling but that didn't work. I couldn't figure out why the counselor wanted me to tell her what was wrong with me (isn't that what she is for?). I left there and went to my family doctor and was prescribed an antidepressant medication. I took this medication hoping that it would cure me from my depression but after a few days, I noticed that I had every side effect it listed. I quit taking it and chose to deal with the depression the best I could. That wasn't the first time I tried medication for depression, a few years earlier I was prescribed an antidepressant. Big mistake! Now don't get me wrong I don't knock anyone who needs antidepressant medication, but when I say big mistake, I literally mean it was a big mistake for me. It made me feel worse. The emotion I was feeling, I attached the name "depression" to it. Although I was feeling what depression describes, it was not depression that I was dealing with. What I was dealing with, were the emotions that come as a result of disobedience to God. I was trying to treat with meds what I should have been treating with obedience. That's why I wasn't having any success using those medications because they were not made to treat symptoms of disobedience and rebellion.

Many of you, just like me, have been misdiagnosed and gone from one extreme to the next trying to cure the symptoms of disobedience and rebellion with something that was not prescribed for it. The only thing that cures disobedience and rebellion is obedience to God. Some of you have been wondering why your symptoms are not getting any better. Could it be that you have been placing a band aid over what needs surgery? Instead of dealing with the real issue, you try to cure your symptoms with shopping, getting a new hair style, jumping into a new relationship, rekindling a past relationship, drinking, smoking, or moving out of town to get a fresh start, going to counseling or perhaps like me, jumping on medication.

You might not like the way you are feeling and to be honest I didn't either. I wanted so bad to get rid of the heaviness and along with jumping on antidepressants, I jumped in and out of more relationships, I partied more, cut and colored my hair, got a weave, went to counseling and the list goes on. I didn't know if I was coming or going. But I never made the connection that the reason I was like this was because of disobedience. Every time I experienced rejection in my relationships, I wanted to take a magic pill that would take the hurt away. The first time I jumped on medication, I shared this information with my boyfriend at the time, because I was looking for sympathy. I was hoping that if he knew I was on antidepressant he would feel sorry and wouldn't reject me. Guess what, I didn't happen that way. Instead it backfired. He told me I was stupid for taking it and it was for crazy people and he laughed at me. His reaction made me feel even worse.

One Christmas morning, while I was still dealing with what I was calling depression, I was sitting at my kitchen table with a glass of pop with ice sitting in front of me. I had never been able to articulate to anyone what I was really feeling on the inside and to be honest, I didn't understand the feelings I was having. The ice had begun to melt and was bobbing around in the glass. As I looked at the ice in the glass, it began to communicate to me, just what I was feeling. As I looked at the ice melt, it helped me understand what I was feeling. The ice was emerged in the pop and like the ice, I felt like I was emerged in water with only my mouth barely exposed, breathing just enough to stay alive. Can you imagine being submerged under water barely able to keep yourself alive? That describes how I felt. I was in a dark place and barely alive. I blamed others and God for my being in this dark place. I felt like life was so unfair. I still didn't make the connection that what I was feeling was the result of my disobedience. I continued to blame everything and everyone.

This behavior continued for about three more years. I have to pause and thank Jesus for His grace and mercy. Looking back over my life, I am just so grateful that he allowed me time to get it together. I just think about those who never got it right and their chance of getting it right had expired. I often wonder, what I could have possibly said on judgment day. NOTHING!!! That is why, it is so important for me to share my testimony, in hopes that you will make the choice to be obedient to God and not suffer the way I did, or miss the opportunity to get it right. I don't want anyone to regret being disobedient and on judgment day, having to give an account.

Needless to say I did not stop having sex outside of marriage. I continued in disobedience for another three years. I totally ignored what God had told me. Whether in a dark place or not, I was determined that I was going to run my life, the way I wanted it to run. In spite of my life spiraling out of control, I continued in sex outside of marriage and idol worship. It was all about me and what I wanted and how I wanted it. Catch this, I was living like this and attending church. I was worshiping both God and idols. Regardless of all the warnings flashing and God's Word being preached, I continued with no fear or remorse.

God's wrath was being unleashed in my life as I continued to operate in physical and spiritual fornication. Although I knew the truth of what God required of me, I held the truth hostage refusing to obey God. *(Romans 1:18)* I'm sure all of us at one time have seen on television a kidnapped victim. The perpetrator ties up and gags the victim and holds them in an isolated place. It is often believed that the kidnapper even though asking for a ransom, does not have intentions of releasing its victim, whether a ransom is paid or not. When it came to the Word of God, I had those same intentions, I knew what God's Word said and held it hostage with no intentions of letting it go. Just like a kidnapper, I gagged and bound the truth with no intent of letting it go. God had spoken to me and I knew what He required of me, but I refused to do it. It scares me while ministering to others and I hear them make excuses for their disobedience. I literally get sick to my stomach and it weighs on me so heavy because I already know what the outcome will be. God's word clearly states in *Galatians 6:7 Be not deceived; God is not mocked: for whatsoever a man soweth, that shall he also reap. (KJV)*

What this clearly means is if you sow (plant) the seed of disobedience you will reap (gather) the penalties of disobedience. I believe while writing this, there are those reading right now who are suffering from the penalties of disobedience. You have for some time now blamed others for your life being in this condition. In the name of Jesus repent and make the choice to no longer choose to operate in disobedience.

I continued in physical fornication by having sex with men I wasn't married to and continued in spiritual fornication by ignoring God and worshipping the relationship by doing whatever it took to keep it together. Even though all the warning signs were there, I still didn't recognize God dealing with me.

The prophet Ezekiel goes on to share with us that the Babylonians came to Aholibah and defiled her.

Ezekiel 23:17 And the Babylonians came to her into the bed of love, and they defiled her with their whoredom, and she was polluted with them, and her mind was alienated from them. **(KJV)**

Aholibah, lusted after and sent for the Babylonians, but after she hooked up with them and opened up her self to them, she didn't know the relationship would come with a price. Because of the hardship that came with the alliance, she grew to dislike them and no longer wanted to be bothered. Sometimes what we think we want is really not what we really want. How many times have you gone after something or someone you wanted really bad? It looked good, smelled good, dressed nice, had money, and had a nice car but after you got it, you soon regretted it.

There are those who just had to have that man, but what you didn't realize, was that man came with a venereal disease, kids, crazy baby momma's, bad credit, no job, a criminal record, no money and plenty of issues. Now after the fact that he has dogged and used you, you find yourself sitting in the seat of regret, thinking, "If I could only turn back the hands of time", wishing you never had done it.

Aholibah no longer wanted to be in a relationship with the Babylonians, instead of realizing her mistakes and looking to God she pushed the envelope even farther when she sought help from Egypt,

Ezekiel 23:18-21 So she discovered her whoredoms, and discovered her nakedness: then my mind was alienated from her, like as my mind was alienated from her sister. 19 Yet she multiplied her whoredoms, in calling to remembrance the days of her youth, wherein she had played the harlot in the land of Egypt. 20 For she doted upon their paramours, whose flesh is as the flesh of asses, and whose issue is like the issue of horses 21 Thus thou calledst to remembrance the lewdness of thy youth, in bruising thy teats by the Egyptians for the paps of thy youth. (KJV)

Aholibah seemed to have forgotten the horrible experience she had with the Egyptians and how they oppressed and mistreated her. Instead, Aholibah got reacquainted by seeking help and placing her confidence in Egypt once again. How familiar does that sound? We sometimes suffer from acute amnesia, by forgetting how crazy and horrible we were treated and end up getting reacquainted with the past experience. Aholibah's whoredom continued to increase as she lusted after the Egyptian paramours (lovers), whose genitals where the size of a donkey and whose emission (semen) was like a horse. This description could suggest the level of enticement and a yearning desire of intimacy with the Egyptian paramours.

Aholibah was driven by lust, with the same intensity that many of us have been driven. The text suggest that Aholibah, was captivated by size and quantity, taking into account that donkeys are known for having very large genitals and horses are known for the large amounts of semen they produce. Some of us have the same characteristics that are found in Aholibah, where we have been infatuated and drawn toward someone or something based on size, quantity and or appearance. I know I have been guilty of going after what looked good or what I thought I could benefit from. Most of us if not all of us, have been driven with the intensity of lust, that once we set our eyes on someone or something, we don't stop until we get it. There are those who don't care who they hurt or step on during the process, while others will even push God away to accomplish what they set out to accomplish and God becomes irrelevant to them (that is until something happens again).

Aholibah chose to repeat her past by choosing to hook back up with the very ones (Egypt) that God had delivered her from. Most, if not all of us, are guilty of this same thing. We have been delivered from a situation but after some time has passed we revisit.   To revisit or get caught back up into something that you have been delivered and set free from, is like a dog who returns to his own vomit. *(Proverbs 26:11)* Who does that? As crazy as it sounds we all have done that at some point in our lives. How many times has God delivered us from crazy relationships or situations and then after some time has passed, just like the dog returning to his vomit, we go right back into the same mess. Take a moment and ponder that thought.

I know we like to think of God as only loving, kind and forgiving, although this is true, the Bible also tells us that God is a jealous God and He is known to unleash His wrath when necessary. Some don't really like to talk about or embrace this side of God, while others act as if this side of God doesn't exist. Aholibah's whoredoms had penalties attached. Aholibah's lovers (the very ones whom she lusted after and joined up with) are the very ones God chose to use as the instrument of her punishment.

Journal

What are some of the ways you have pushed the envelope with God?

What has been your result of not staying within the boundaries?

Now that you have recognized your faults, how do you plan to move forward?

Chapter 6 - Consequence

There's an old saying "If you play with fire you'll get burned". This was meant to be understood, in the sense that if you fool around with someone or something that is forbidden and potentially dangerous or harmful, expect to suffer the consequences. Fire, although it can be attractive and mesmerizing, is hot, dangerous and can be fatal.

In this next passage of scripture, Ezekiel shares with us, the consequence that God passes onto Aholibah, as a result of the mounting evidence He has against her. She stands now convicted and God is executing punishment as result of her disobedience.

Ezek: 23:22-24 **Therefore, O Aholibah, thus saith the Lord GOD; Behold, I will raise up thy lovers against thee, from whom thy mind is alienated, and I will bring them against thee on every side; 23 The Babylonians, and all the Chaldeans, Pekod, and Shoa, and Koa, and all the Assyrians with them: all of them desirable young men, captains and rulers, great lords and renowned, all of them riding upon horses. 24 And they shall come against thee with chariots, wagons, and wheels, and with an** *assembly of people, which shall set against thee buckler and shield and helmet round about: and I will set judgment before them, and they shall judge thee according to their judgments. (KJV)*

God has now employed the very ones she lusted after, admired and just had to have, as the tool to execute judgment against her. He used the very ones she hooked up with and couldn't get enough of. The very ones that Aholibah lusted after, only to find, that after she got what she thought she wanted, her lust turned quickly into hatred. This reminds me of how we go after people and things that go against the will and way of God only to find that once we get what we think we want, we soon find out, that our lust has turned to hatred. I know I'm not by myself, when I say that I have sought after a relationship, that I just knew would make me happy, only to find out later, that it wasn't what I thought or hoped it to be. I found myself, miserable, unstable, feeling half crazy, well, really all the way crazy, not knowing half the time if I was coming or going. I was so consumed with the relationship, that I didn't even recognize how dumb I was being or sounding. I notice in my relationships that in the beginning, they seemed to start off good, but once my feelings got real deep, that's when the relationship went south (down the drain). My disobedience and rebellion caused me to suffer the consequence of God's wrath (His anger). I shared in chapter two, that God is a jealous God. *(Exodus 34:14)* He does not want us to worship anything or anyone but Him. When I refused to obey God, I placed my will and way above God. Placing my will and way above God, led me into idol worship.

God had called me out of fornication and like I previously shared, I had refused to come out. I worship the relationship (idol) rather than worshipping God. The red lights were flashing and warnings signs were going up all around me, clearly telling me to stop. When one relationship would fall apart, instead of stopping long enough to access my situation, I continued to seek relationship after relationship and found myself in a downward spiral. My remedy for a failed relationship was to replace it with another. A secular artist made a song called "Irreplaceable". Had that song been out back then, I would have used that as my theme song, especially the part of the song that goes like this "you must not know bout me, you must not know bout me, I can have another you in a minute matter fact he'll be here in a minute baby." That verse is about replacing one failed relationship with another one (that's exactly what many of us do). Instead of yielding to what God was calling me to do, I just continued replacing them.

Depicted in detail, God told Aholibah that His jealousy was set against her and the enemy would deal furiously with her. He goes on to say that her nose and ears would be taken away and what is left (remnant and residue) will be destroyed and her children would be carried away as part of her punishment.

Ezekiel 23:25 And I will set my jealousy against thee, and they shall deal furiously with thee: they shall take away thy nose and thine ears; and thy remnant shall fall by the sword: they shall take thy sons and thy daughters; and thy residue shall be devoured by the fire. (KJV)

Most scholars suggest that figuratively the nose and ears represent Jerusalem's leadership (The King and Priest). Jerusalem would no longer have a King to lead or a Priest to bring forth the Word of God, which would be detrimental for anyone in this situation. There are other scholars who believe that the nose and ears represent a custom practice where an adulteress wife, would be mutilated by the cutting off of her nose and ears for breaking her vows. This could suggest that God spoke this parable to show Aholibah (Jerusalem), her fate being the same as an adulteress wife, according to the nation's customs and practices whom she had previously intermingled with. It is believed that mutilating an adulteress wife by cutting off her nose and ears was practiced among the Egyptians, Persians, and Chaldeans.

God also states that her children will be taken away. The decisions we make, affect our children and others around us. Notice the children were carried away. The text does not suggest that the children did anything wrong, but were taken as a result of the parent's sin. Please hear me; we are not the only ones who are affected by our sins. The text states that the children were carried away.

We are often so busy caught up in doing our own thing that the enemy (satan) is carrying our children away physically and spiritually. They are carried away physically into roles that they were not ready for. Some children have been carried away and forced to grow up fast because of the lack of proper guidance and supervision. They have been left to run the house and look out for their siblings because momma is doing her own thing. Then there are those who are carried away and left in the care of other people (foster care, babysitters or other relatives). Then there are those who are carried away mentally and dealing with the scars of rejection of having been left to look out for their self or left in the company of an abuser. Some children that are carried away end up falling into the same cycle as their parents. It's not only about us and the mentality of "I'm doing me." Our actions bring consequences that affect not only us but our children and others too.

Journal

Are you playing with fire?

Does God have enough evidence against you for a conviction?

Do you believe there are consequences to your sin?

Are you willing to suffer the consequence of your sin?

Chapter 7 – Broke & Naked On Front Street

Who wishes to be broke? I can't imagine anyone waking up in the morning trying to figure out how to be broke. There are many reasons why people are broke, whether it is from lack of employment, having to help out other people or living beyond their means. Another reason someone could end up broke, is by falling victim to theft. There is nothing worse than working hard, only to have your money, retirement and or valuables, stolen from you. Here in the text we find God declaring that He will hand (give) Aholibah (Jerusalem) over to their enemies and describes the kind of treatment they would receive. He continues to share how they will take away everything they have worked for, leaving them broke, naked and bare (disgraced and embarrassed) for everyone to see.

> *Ezekiel 23:26-29 They shall also strip thee out of thy clothes, and take away thy fair jewels. 27 Thus will I make thy lewdness to cease from thee, and thy whoredom brought from the land of Egypt: so that thou shalt not lift up thine eyes unto them, nor remember Egypt any more.* **(KJV)**

We must be careful not to use the provisions that God provides us, to employ sin. God stripped the jewels and clothes that Aholibah used to attract the Assyrians and Babylonians to hook up with her. By doing this God caused her to stop and never to remember Egypt (where she learned her lewdness and whoredoms).

> *Ezekiel 23: 28-29 For thus saith the Lord GOD; Behold, I will deliver thee into the hand of them whom thou hatest, into the hand of them from whom thy mind is alienated: 29 And they shall deal with thee hatefully, and shall take away all thy labour, and shall leave thee naked and bare: and the nakedness of thy whoredoms shall be discovered, both thy lewdness and thy whoredoms. (KJV)*

God explains that this would happen as the result of their disobedience. This helps us to understand that in the same sense, it is possible for us to lose everything we have and everything we worked for as a result of our disobedience. I can testify that I suffered many losses as a result of my own disobedience. I went into debt and lost my house and almost lost my mind. God continues to share that not only will Aholibah's (Jerusalem) enemies take away everything she worked for; they will also leave them naked and bare and for all to see. (*Ezekiel 23:29*)

Have you ever stepped out of the shower or bathtub or maybe even been sitting on the toilet, when someone comes busting in and there you are naked and exposed, trying desperately to cover yourself? I remember an experience I had in a public bathroom facility. I thought I could hurry and use the restroom without locking the stall door. Big mistake! Before I knew it someone pushed opened the door and there I was with my pants down, trying desperately to cover myself. This experience was so embarrassing to me. Who wants to be caught with their pants down? There are some people who are comfortable in their nakedness; they walk around nude without any problem, but most of us are not comfortable being exposed to the world.

This reminds me of an experience I had in Jamaica. The first time I went to Jamaica was with my cousins and I have to say that it was one of my favorite vacations. My second day there was very interesting I might add. There I was laying out on the beach, kicking it with my cousin, tossing back a few Red Stripes (Jamaican beer) and bam, out of nowhere, no warning at all, I see women walking around topless. I turned to one of my cousins in shock and her response was, "Oh, they do that down here, it's legal." That tripped me out but get this, later and after a few Red Stripes and being two sheets in the wind (tipsy), I convinced myself to go topless and guess what? I did it. Although I had a buzz (tipsy), I still felt a little uncomfortable and it wasn't long before I put my bathing suit top back on. Even though the alcohol gave me the courage to remove my top, the alcohol could not keep me from becoming uncomfortable in my nakedness.

Some of us are familiar with the term "Put On Front Street". Although the younger generation used the term "On Blast" while others use the term "Called Out". Even though we have different ways of articulating an expression, what all of these terms really mean, is to get embarrassed in front of others. The text shared that Aholibah's enemies would leave her naked and bare for everyone to see. When her enemies uncovered her nakedness, she was put "On Front Street". Several of us like our girl Aholibah, have been put "On Front Street" where we have experienced some very embarrassing moments. One of my many embarrassing "On Blast" moments was, when I experienced a type of nakedness that didn't involve the removal of my physical clothing. This is what I like to call the nakedness of embarrassment, of being stripped of a relationship.

Like I shared earlier, I disobeyed God by refusing to stop having sex outside of marriage. I told God that it would be okay for me to continue because we were getting married. Everything seemed okay. My excuse seemed to have pacified Him because I was no longer hearing Him speak to me (so I thought). I was planning my wedding and after a couple of months of planning, out of nowhere, tragedy struck and I was left stripped of the relationship, naked, embarrassed and humiliated and "On Front Street" for everyone to see. God gives us opportunity to correct our behavior before He takes action. He had told me to come out of fornication and I refused to listen and as a result I had to suffer the consequences of embarrassment of being left at the altar and left having to explain why I was no longer getting married. Aholibah had the opportunity to correct her behavior before God put her "On Blast".

Have you ever experienced, the "Talk" (explaining why you were being disciplined) that your parents would give you before implementing the discipline. I grew up in a household where discipline was carried out. My parent's belief was not in sparing (withholding correction) the rod. One of the things that I hated equal to being disciplined was the "Talk" that took place, before, during and even after being disciplined, to explain why you were being disciplined. I don't know about you, but as a kid, I wasn't interested in the reasons why, I just wanted to get it over with. Here we see God giving the "Talk" giving the reasons for the punishment.

> *Ezekiel 23:30-31 I will do these things unto thee, because thou hast gone a whoring after the heathen, and because thou art polluted with their idols. 31Thou hast walked in the way of thy sister; therefore will I give her cup into thine hand. (KJV)*

God gives us opportunity to correct our behavior before He takes action. He had told me to come out of fornication and I refused to listen and as a result I had to suffer the consequences. Aholibah watched her sister reap what she had sown and instead of heeding the warning she chose to take the same path and suffered the same consequences.

Journal

What are some things you noticed you have lost because of your sin?

Have you suffered embarrassment because of your sin?

Are you willing to correct your behavior before God takes action?

Chapter 8 – What Goes Around, Comes Around

For every event that occurs, there follows another event, as the result of the first event, that has either a pleasant or unpleasant outcome. A more memorable term that I am familiar with is "What Goes Around Comes Around". This is a term that also describes what happens with a person's actions. Whatever you do in life to other people, whether good or bad, the same will return to you. The basic nature of God's Justice is the law of sowing and reaping found *in Galatians 6:7* Be *not deceived; God is not mocked: for whatsoever a man soweth, that shall he also reap."* From a spiritual context, the idea of reaping and sowing is to expect to harvest the fruit of your behavior, just as farmers expect to harvest the crops that they plant.

Here in the text, God is implementing His law of reaping and sowing. God is saying that Aholibah, will drink of her sister's cup, which is deep and large and she would be laughed at and ridiculed.

Ezekiel 23:32 Thus saith the Lord GOD; Thou shalt drink of thy sister's cup deep and large: thou shalt be laughed to scorn and had in derision; it containeth much. (KJV)

Aholibah's fate would now be the same as her sister's fate. Aholibah had to drink of the same cup of her sister. God had already dealt with the sins of Aholah and now Aholibah will reap the same degree of punishment as her sister. Aholibah would be laughed to scorn for God's punishment is deep and large. The cup of the Lord's vengeance holds a large quantity. The content of this cup is not designed for enjoyment. Aholibah is not given a choice to drink from this cup but she is being forced. This reminds me of being a kid and being forced to do what my parents said. When my mom made dinner, I and my brother had to eat what she made. We were not offered any options, unlike kids today. I always dreaded when she made lima beans. No matter how much I complained about the horrible taste, I still had to eat them. I also hated waking up early to go to church every Sunday but again, I had no option. Aholibah, I'm sure, didn't want to drink of her sister's cup but she had to. Aholibah had to reap the consequence of what she had sown.

Everything that we do has repercussions. Whether we choose to believe it or not, the choices we make, do come back to us one way or another. We cannot escape the consequences of our actions. We should continue to watch the way we live our lives because Galatians 6:7, tells us that God cannot be mocked. He sees it all and we will reap what we have sown. It has been said that if you sow a thought you reap an act. Sow an act, you reap a habit. Sow a habit, you reap a character. Sow a character, you reap a consequence. What it all boils down to is this, your deeds, good or bad, will repay you. The book of Job says it best. Job said that those whom devise trouble and plant wickedness get the same in return. *(Job 4:8)*

Aholibah's fate is the likeness of someone intoxicated. The cup that she has to drink is filled with God's wrath and fury (anger). This cup will cause her to become intoxicated with grief, sorrow and anguish. She will become so uncomfortable and will not be able to shake it.

> *Ezekiel 23:33 Thou shalt be filled with drunkenness and sorrow, with the cup of astonishment and desolation, with the cup of thy sister Samaria. (KJV)*

There are many sobering methods that are only myths. Drinking coffee, cold showers, and drinking water or eating bread to sober up is only a myth. The only thing other than medical intervention that will cure intoxication is time. There are no quick fixes. Aholibah had to drink from the cup of desolation (devastation) and astonishment (overpowering wonder). Intoxicated with her portion of misery, sorrow and devastation, would suggest that she had no sense of reasoning and could not make head or tails of anything, staggering around as a drunkard, sick and ready to fall.

It wasn't until I quit drinking that I realized how ridiculous, obnoxious and nerve wracking a person is while drunk. Their words become slurred, they stagger around, they're loud and not to mention their breath stinks. We can only imagine how ridiculous and sad, Aholibah looked in her drunkenness. I wonder was she hurling insults at those who watched. I bet she picked fights with those she came in contact with. I can definitely relate to that. Sometimes we don't recognize right away that we are suffering the consequences of our actions. That's when we begin to go on a rampage in our drunken state staggering around looking ridiculous, hurling insults, and picking fights and blaming other people, not recognizing that we brought the punishment on ourselves.

"Finish your plate" has been echoed throughout many households. My brother and I were raised in an era where we could not leave the table until our plates were cleaned. There was no such thing as wasting food, at least not in our household. My mom would always say "There are people in Africa starving to death." God told Aholibah to not only drink from the cup but she had to finish it. She didn't have the option of leaving any behind.

Ezekiel 23:34 Thou shalt even drink it and suck it out, and thou shalt break the sherds thereof, and pluck off thine own breasts: for I have spoken it, saith the Lord GOD.

The text suggests that what was in the cup was so bad that it would cause Aholibah to pluck off her breast (to inflict pain upon herself). I definitely can relate. When God was dealing with my disobedience of refusing to come out of fornication and because of the bitterness, misery and heaviness I was experiencing, I began to beat myself up with words of destruction. I tore down my self esteem, I wouldn't fix myself up, and I wasn't eating or getting the proper amount of sleep. After God told Aholibah, her fate, He said "for I have spoken it, saith the Lord God." When God speaks something He means it. There is no reversal. God said that His Word will not return unto Him void, but it shall accomplish what it was sent to do. *Isaiah 55:11*

God said that because Aholibah forgot Him and cast Him behind her back, she has to accept the responsibility of her wickedness.

103

Ezekiel 23:35 Therefore thus saith the Lord GOD; Because thou hast forgotten me, and cast me behind thy back, therefore bear thou also thy lewdness and thy whoredoms. (KJV)

Forgetting God and going on with our own thing, causes us to mock (turn our nose up and disregarding and not believing God). God said, "Be not deceived (fooled); God is not mocked". We mock God when we take for granted that His eyes have been on us all along. We also mock Him when we discard Him like trash and treat Him like He's not relevant and having the "I'm doing me"attitude. It goes on to say, for whatsoever a man soweth that also shall he reap *Galatians 6:7*. When we forget and turn our backs on God, we need to be ready to accept the responsibility of our own wickedness, by reaping what we have sown.

Journal

Are you reaping what you have sown?

Have you cast God behind your back?

Are you mocking God, by believing that your sin will not be dealt with?

Is or has it been worth it?

Chapter 9 - Lukewarm

After Aholah (Israel) had been taken captive, those that were left, integrated with Judah (Aholibah) and settled in Jerusalem becoming one nation. Here in this passage the prophet Ezekiel is speaking now jointly, to the two sisters, Aholah (the remnant of Israel) and Aholibah (Jerusalem). God told Ezekiel to declare unto them their abominations that include idolatry, (the shedding of innocent blood by sacrificing their sons) and adultery (worshiping idols).

Ezekiel 23:36-39 The LORD said moreover unto me; Son of man, wilt thou judge Aholah and Aholibah? yea, declare unto them their abominations; 37 That they have committed adultery, and blood is in their hands, and with their idols have they committed adultery, and have also caused their sons, whom they bare unto me, to pass for them through the fire, to devour them. 38 Moreover this they have done unto me: they have defiled my sanctuary in the same day, and have profaned my Sabbaths. 39 For when they had slain their children to their idols, then they came the same day into my sanctuary to profane it; and, lo, thus have they done in the midst of mine house. (KJV)

In addition to the list of their abominations, the text

suggests that on the same day that they committed these awful acts, they came into God's sanctuary and profaned (disrespected) His Sabbaths which was a direct insult to God. Imagine your car running out of gas on a hot 90 degree day and having to walk three miles to the nearest gas station. Upon your arrival with sweat rolling down your forehead and back, you spot a water fountain and reach down and began to take a drink and are caught totally off guard because the water is lukewarm. Yuck!!! Who wants lukewarm water, especially on a hot summer day? I've come across a few water fountains like that and each time the water was warm, I spit it out and walked away disappointed.

In the book of Revelation God is speaking to the church of the Laodiceans. God said that He knows their actions and they are neither hot nor cold. He also states that He wishes they were hot or cold. God goes on to say that because they are lukewarm neither hot or cold; He would spit them out of His mouth. (Revelation 3:15, 16) God was not pleased with the Laodiceans, because they were not fully committed to Him. The analogy God uses, suggest that He is disgusted, in those who are lukewarm (not fully committed) and will reject them. This is very relevant for us today. God wants us to be fully committed to Him. There are no in between when it comes to God.

He wants all or nothing. He doesn't want half of us, He wants it all. We're either going to be for Him or against Him. God gives us the choice of being hot or cold but doesn't give us the option of lukewarm. The intent for hot, is to be fully committed and cold symbolizes the unbeliever. There are those, who like myself, would ask why God would even suggest being cold (unbeliever). Some scholars suggest that those who are cold have no disguise or concealment; they are just straight up but there is still a chance that they could be converted.

There is a way that seems right to a man, but the end of that way is death. (Proverbs 16:25) Those who are lukewarm, profess to be a Christian, without any evidence of sanctification (set apart for God's use) or holiness (purity, free from sin). When someone is lukewarm they are blinded by delusion and lack the sincerity of true conversion. Efforts made to reach this person is rejected by many excuses some being "God knows my heart", or "only God can judge me". Being lukewarm also causes one to never apply the truth to their self. They become so consumed with thinking all is well and that they are safe but without any concern about their soul. Let's take a minute and talk, I mean really talk. Would you be okay with having a boyfriend or husband that was half committed? Would you be cool with him being half with you and half with someone else? Most of us would not be down with that. We should feel the same when it comes to our commitment to God.

Aholah and Aholibah, represents the lukewarm analogy. They're neither hot nor cold. They had to be pretty bold to come into God's sanctuary on the same day that they had slain their children to idols. This was grimy to say the least, but truthfully this is done in some sense today. In the past, I was definitely guilty of trying to worship both God and idols. There were times that I came strutting into the sanctuary after a night of partying, drinking and at times having sexual intercourse with someone who was not my spouse. Oh wait; I just remembered something real crazy. On a couple of occasions, I brought with me, the guy that God had told me to stop fornicating with. At that time in my life, I didn't care. I didn't see anything wrong with it. My philosophy was this; no matter what I did or how bad it was, as long as I made it to church, that was good enough for me. Not only is that grimy, it clearly showed that I had no respect for God or His place of worship.

Church attendance only is not enough. God wants us to serve Him and Him only. He wants us to dedicate ourselves to Him. He doesn't want us to come before Him any kind of way. He requires that we come before Him in a holy and pleasing way. Yes, it is true, we are not perfect beings, but we should be striving daily to become better. God requires us to present (dedicate) ourselves to Him. What this says is that in presenting ourselves, we communicate to God, that we are giving up our will and way to accept His will and way. (*Romans 12*)

The text allows us to see God's displeasure of the disrespect Aholah and Aholibah displayed in His sanctuary and towards His Sabbaths and I'm sure He is equally displeased with us when we disrespect His sanctuary and Sabbath with our own sins. (*Jeremiah 7:9-10*) Do we really think that God doesn't notice? Do we really think its okay? God continues to share that Aholibah sent for men to come and dressed herself up for them and took what was meant for God and used it on them, in addition to what she had already done.

> *Ezekiel 23: 40-42 And furthermore, that ye have sent for men to come from far, unto whom a messenger was sent; and, lo, they came: for whom thou didst wash thyself, paintedst thy eyes, and deckedst thyself with ornaments, (KJV)*

No one forced Aholibah, nor did these men come looking for her, no, she sent for them. How many times have we been guilty of this same thing? How many of us sent for the man, or sent a message by someone else, that later caused us some major issues. God also shares that Aholibah took God's provisions and spent it on these men

> *Ezekiel 23:41 And satest upon a stately bed, and a table prepared before it, whereupon thou hast set mine incense and mine oil. (KJV)*

The text suggest that great preparation was made for these men. Aholibah sat upon a stately bed and a table was prepared. It is suggested by some scholars that this table was a replica of the Damascus altar, where she set the oil and incense that was normally used to worship God. This same thing is done even today. There are some who take God's provisions and use them on everything and everybody but Him. When I committed fornication, I took my body which was meant for God and gave it to someone else or when I took the house that God blessed me with and did things in it that were not pleasing to Him. The text also suggest that Aholibah furnished the spot and was willing to allow these men the freedom to exercise their idol worship around her even though it went against the law of God.

> *Ezekiel 23:42 And a voice of a multitude being at*

ease was with her: and with the men of the common sort were brought Sabeans from the wilderness, which put bracelets upon their hands, and beautiful crowns upon their heads. (KJV)

Not only did Aholibah furnish the spot, these men seemed to be at ease. To be at ease is when someone is comfortable, relieved and content. These men were at ease with her. It's apparent; she was looking out for their best interest. Most of us can relate to preparing an environment for someone to be at ease. There are some women who set their homes up, based on a man's wants and needs. They will buy certain groceries, beer, liquor, drugs, shoes and clothes. Then there are those who will even go as far as buying play stations and other game units, just to keep them entertained. Let's not forget those who will let a man use their car and give them full access to their bank account. These are situation that some women create just to have the man feel comfortable and content.

Here in this next passage of scripture, we find that Aholibah has not learned her lesson she continued to play the harlot.

Ezekiel 23:43 Then said I unto her that was old in adulteries, Will they now commit whoredoms with her, and she with them? 44

112

Yet they went in unto her, as they go in unto a woman that playeth the harlot: so went they in unto Aholah and unto Aholibah, the lewd women. 45 And the righteous men, they shall judge them after the manner of adulteresses, and after the manner of women that shed blood; because they are adulteresses, and blood is in their hands. (KJV)

You would think that the experience of the situation would cause Aholibah to access the situation and finally get to a place where she can say "enough is enough" "this is getting old" It's time for a change.

Journal

Are you lukewarm?

Are you comfortable in your current situation?

Who are you trying to please?

Have you learned your lesson?

Are you at a place where you are saying enough is enough?

Chapter 10 - Made an Example of

Recently, a teacher in the Ohio educational system was made an example of and sentenced to two years in jail and three years probation, for enrolling and allowing her children to attend a school that was not in her district. Some people, me included, felt this punishment was extreme, considering the nature of the offense. The Ohio School district for whatever reason, felt she needed to be prosecuted. It is some people's opinion that she was clearly made an example of, with considering the punishment she received.

In this passage of scripture, we can see Aholibah being made an example of.

Ezekiel 23:46-49 For thus saith the Lord GOD; I will bring up a company upon them, and will give them to be removed and spoiled. 47 And the company shall stone them with stones, and dispatch them with their swords; they shall slay their sons and their daughters, and burn up their houses with fire 48 Thus will I cause lewdness to cease out of the land, that all women may be taught not to do after your lewdness. 49 And they shall recompense your lewdness upon you, and ye shall bear the sins of your idols: and ye shall know that I am the

Lord GOD. (KJV)

God is executing judgment against Aholah and Aholibah, using the Babylonians as instrument of destruction. Because of their adultery, they are being stoned under the law of adultery found in *(Leviticus 20.10, Deuteronomy 22:22 and John 8:3)*. God also states that as a result of this destruction, He will cause their wickedness to come to an end, so that all women will be taught a lesson, not to repeat the same behavior. God goes on to point out that they will suffer for their sins and they will know that He is Lord God.

It is the testimony of others that allows us to learn and keep from making the same mistakes. That is one of the reasons why I wanted to share my testimony in this book. I don't want anyone to make the same mistakes that I made. I'm sure the teacher who enrolled her children in the unauthorized school district, never in a million years, thought she'd be suffering the consequences for doing so. Because of her actions, she is now made an example of, so that others might be taught not to follow the same path.

Journal

How have you been made an example?

Have you learned from others mistakes?

Are you willing to change?

Chapter 11 - Get It, Before It Gets You

I lived in a state of rebellion for a long time and suffered the consequences of it. It wasn't until I sat under the teaching of my former Pastor, Bishop Timothy Clark that I was taught the importance of sanctification (set apart for God's use) and holiness (sacred and devoted to God). As I continued to sit under Bishop Clark's teaching, I became sin conscious, but I still wasn't fully surrendered to God. I had reached a point in my life where I allowed God to be Lord over certain areas of my life but not all of it. I wasn't willing to allow Him to be Lord over my sex and love life. I felt like I had that area of my life under control. It seemed like everything was coming together in my life. I was attending church regularly and I enjoyed bible study. I was cool with following God's word all the way up to where it talks about fornication. I ignored that part. Whenever fornication was mentioned, I just ignored it. I knew it was wrong according to God's word but I just refused to stop. I actually thought it was impossible to do. I wondered how a relationship would even last without having sex. I also felt like God was being unreasonable and didn't really understand what is was like to be human and I felt like His expectations were ridiculous and unattainable. Did He really intend for us to follow His entire word?

I would have never thought in a million years, that the encouragement and support I had given to someone, would soon lead to my own deliverance.

One Saturday morning during the spring of 2005, I was having a conversation with someone and during that conversation; she shared with me all the hardships and loss she had suffered. During the conversation she revealed that she felt, that this happened as a result of her disobedience. She told me that God, had told her to go to this particular church and she didn't go. After hearing all the losses she incurred, I immediately told her, "If God told you to do something you need to do it." I went on to say, "I don't care how long ago He told you to do it, you still need to do it." I could tell from our conversation she knew she needed to do it, but I also felt like she was scared so I told her I would go with her. Even though this was not my issue, I sensed urgency about it. It felt like her situation would worsen if she continued to refuse to do what God had told her to do. Although I recognized what she needed to do, I had not recognized what I needed to do. It's funny how we can see what's going on in other people's life and give advice, but not recognize or refuse to recognize our own issues. We are so quick to dish out advice but not prepared to take the same advice and apply it to our own situation.

The next morning we met at the church. I was so happy that she was finally doing what God had told her to do and I was equally happy to be there to support her. After arriving at the church and being seated, I could tell she was happy about finally deciding to come. When the preacher stood up, I was caught off guard by his sermon topic. It was entitled "Get it before It Gets you". As he began to preach, he warned the congregation to come out of the sin we were in, before it ultimately destroys us. As he continued to preach, my mind wandered and I began complaining to God about my teenage daughter being sexually active. God began to speak to me but not in the way that I thought He would. I sat in church complaining to God, asking Him to fix her and as I mentioned before, instead of fixing her, He began to check me (deal with my issues). God basically told me that my sexual sin was no different than hers. I tried to argue the age difference, that didn't fly with God. God said sin is sin no matter the age. Every time I pointed out her issue, He pointed back at me. God was calling me for the second time out of fornication. I told God that it was impossible to be in a relationship or get married without having sex first. I also told Him that nobody would want me if I stopped having sex. God's response was "Don't nobody want you anyway" and "No one has come to stay". I have to admit, I was so embarrassed by what God was saying. Even though this conversation was going on internally, I felt like everyone in the church could hear Him speaking to me. What God was saying to me was painfully true, no one came to stay and no one married me. There's an old saying "why buy the cow when the milk is free." God continued with the conversation by saying this, "If you give it up they ain't going to want you." and "If you don't give it up they ain't going to want you." What God was saying was this, if they ain't going to want you, wouldn't it be better not to give it up than to give it up and they still don't want you. That made sense to me and that very moment I made the choice to come out of fornication.

After that encounter with God, my life changed. I instantly made the decision to obey God. I did it without having all the answers right then and there but all I knew was that I needed to obey. This was the second time He had told me to come out of fornication. I felt a type of urgency attached to what God was calling me out of. I sensed that my life would be destroyed if I failed to obey God. I knew I needed to Get It (sin) Before It Got me (destroyed me). Although I made the decision to yield to God's will and way, I still had some questions but I was cool

121

with moving forward.

After leaving church, I spent a lot of time alone, just thinking and processing the sermon and the conversation I had with God. Like I mentioned before, I still had some questions. As I processed things, I began to wonder was I the only one God told to do this because it didn't seem like He was addressing anyone else. I also knew I wanted to get married but I still didn't think it was possible without having sex first. So many thoughts flooded my mind that I became so consumed and overwhelmed, wondering if I was the only one on the planet that God had asked to do this. Everyone I knew was having sex and doing what they do, but now I felt like an odd ball. At this point, I was obeying God out of fear of what might happen to me. The only way I can articulate what I was feeling was, it was like God had punked me (forced me) into becoming celibate and I had chosen to obey out of fear.

I was starting to feel like I was the only one on the planet who was celibate. I was so consumed with this thought that it was taking a toll on me. I could not shake the thoughts flooding my brain so, out of desperation, I cornered a non-married Christian female co-worker who just so happened to be a minister. I had to ask if she was celibate and how she manages being celibate and any challenges she had. For those who know me, know I can be very blunt. Instead of dancing around the subject, I just came on out and asked her was she celibate. I think initially she was in shock because of my direct approach but soon after, she recognized I was not playing but truly in need of some answers. I will never forget how I corned her in front of the women's restroom, without first saying hi or hello. I just cut through the chase and asked the question. She was very honest and shared her testimony about her initial struggle with fornication and how she was delivered from it. Hearing her testimony helped me so much, it allowed me to realize that I was not the only one.

I was still obeying God out of fear until I began studying the book of Hosea. The details of the first three chapters of this book describe the marriage between Hosea and his unfaithful wife Gomer. Their marriage was used as an example to describe God's (faithful husband) love for the nation of Israel (unfaithful wife).

God told Hosea to marry Gomer, an adulterous woman because the land (Israel) he was living in, was guilty of adultery for departing from God. Hosea did what God told him to do and married her. (*Hosea 1*) The text suggests that Gomer had been involved with other men while married to Hosea, but God told Hosea to show her love in spite of her infidelity. God tells him to love her as He has loved the Israelites even though they served other gods. (*Hosea 3:1*) This text also mirrors what we discussed in the previous chapters surrounding the two sisters Aholah (Israel) and Aholibah (Judah) and their unfaithfulness.

God said that Israel was not His wife. (*Hosea 2:2*) It's obvious as to why God would make this statement. It is my opinion that He was ashamed of her because of her unfaithfulness. Who wants to be married to someone who is unfaithful? Even people who are just dating expect the other person to be faithful. God said that unless she stops her adultery and unfaithfulness, He would strip everything from her. He goes on to say, He will block her path and block her from finding her way. God also said that Gomer will chase after her lovers but not find them. (*Hosea 2:7*) This sounded so familiar to me. Like I shared previously regarding my relationships, I kept seeking after them but they were not working out. No matter how hard I tried or how much I switched up my methods, the relationships continued to fail. All along I had thought that the other person was to blame for the relationship not working. But here it allowed me to understand that God was the one who was stopping it. I was in the same position that

Gomer was in. Because of my unfaithfulness (rebellion), God was stripping me and blocking my path.

God states that after He stripped her and blocked her path, she decided that she would return back to Him but she had not acknowledged that God was the one who provided for her. *(Hosea 2:7-8)* I was the poster child for this idea. I was a pro at running to God when things didn't work out for me. If things weren't going right in my life, I ran to church. I was there faithfully when I went through a break up and when my world was falling apart. I would call on God in prayer and I would read the Bible when things were going wrong. I even got other people involved in this. I would call up other people to pray for me. During this time of my life, I should have gotten an Oscar for the best actress when it came to being a faithful Christian.

Even though I thought going to church was cool, I still didn't acknowledge God's purpose and position in my life. I treated God as a rebound. I was with Him only until something I thought was better came along or when life was going good. Can you imagine how that must have felt to God? Can you imagine being someone's second thought, second choice or second best? How would you feel to know that someone just settled for you because they didn't have any other choice at the time? Wouldn't you feel used? Well, that's exactly what I did. I treated God as second best. Not recognizing God's true purpose and His position in our life can cause us to suffer great losses. God said that because Israel didn't recognize Him as her provider that He would take away everything He provided her with. *(Hosea 2:8-13)* God not only said He would take everything away. God said that He would take away His grain when it ripens and the new wine when it is ready. The text suggests that she will see God's provisions (the grain and new wine) but not be able to benefit from them. The text also suggest that He will even take back the wool and linen intended to cover her nakedness, which suggests that she already had this in her possession. So not only would He allow her to see what she could have had (grain and new wine), He even takes what she already has. Now that's deep isn't it?

When we are unfaithful to God, He will not only allow us to see what blessings we could have had, He also takes what we have and there is nothing we or anyone else can do to stop Him. God said that no one would be able to take her out of His hands. The text suggests that no one can stop God from doing what He wants to do. No matter how hard we try to reverse the effects of what God is doing in our life or in the life of someone else, this allows us to know that we will not be successful. *(Hosea 2:10)* God continues to share how He will punish her and lead her into the desert and speak kindly to her. *(Hosea 2:14)* This suggests that God is not interested in just punishing her (Israel), He is leading her into the desert place (of correction and sole dependency) to speak to her heart. This shows us that God will usher us into a desert place, a solitary, dry, empty and unproductive place in our lives because that's the place that He can fully get our attention and to speak to our heart. To be totally honest, most of us are not willing to listen to God until we are in a place where we are empty and unfulfilled, having nothing left. Then there are some who are in a desert place and not open to allowing God to speak to their heart and tend to blame others or seek to find their own solution which is never successful.

God's desire is to restore us where we need to be in Him. He is waiting for us to love Him as He has patiently and unconditionally loved us. I saw myself as Gomer and the nation Israel. I was always running after everything but God. As soon as I got rejected, dogged, used or got in trouble, I came running back, until another opportunity presented itself. I had a habit of doing this. It wasn't until I read how Hosea loved Gomer unconditionally, regardless of all the things she had done. This helps me to understand my relationship between me and God. He loved me so much that, even though I was unfaithful to Him, He continued to love me unconditionally and wanted to reconcile our relationship. He led me through my own personal desert place in order to deal with my issues and speak to my heart. I didn't like being in a desert place. I was miserable and very uncomfortable. I didn't understand it at first and yes, I blamed God and other people for my misery but God refused to throw me away. Although God was angered by my disobedience, He continued to love me. He was not willing to allow me to be estranged any longer. The consequence of my disobedience was used as a tool of correction. God's intent was not to destroy me but to restore me back to Him.

Get **It** before **It** Gets You is so important. God wants us to deal with the sin in our lives. He wants us to deal with it before it ultimately destroys us. He has given us time to get it together. He is not interested in lip service; He wants us to take action. God is calling us out of the unfaithfulness of participating in things that are contrary to His Word.

Maybe your **It** is not fornication, but whatever your **It** is, you need to "Get **It** Before **It** Gets You"! Disobedience to God's word is very dangerous and has consequences that can lead to destruction. Aholah and Aholibah showed us that God will deal with our disobedience.

God told Hosea to go show his love for his unfaithful wife. (*Hosea 3:1*) Notice, God didn't say wait until Gomer got herself together. He told Hosea to love her even though she is an adulteress. God loves and cares for us so much that He doesn't withhold His love until we get it together. Hosea had to buy back Gomer. The text proposes that Gomer must have been bought as a slave or was hired out. Hosea redeemed Gomer in order for her to regain her freedom. Jesus redeemed us all with the shedding of His precious blood on The Cross of Calvary. We were bought with a price. We belong to God and we have a duty to be faithful to Him. After Hosea redeemed Gomer, he gave her instructions on how to live as his wife. (*Hosea 3:2-3*) God's word gives us instruction on how we are to live. It is the blue print to the do's and dont's of life.

I'm sure Hosea endured a broken heart, embarrassment, scorn and ridicule for marrying such a woman but it didn't stop him from doing what God told him to do. God's purpose for Hosea marrying Gomer was to show that Israel was guilty of adultery in departing from God. Most scholars believe that the purpose of this message for us today is to wake us up and recognize our need for deliverance. It shows us that God stands ready to forgive and restore anyone who is willing to repent (turn away from sin). Today just like the nation of Israel we have failed to demonstrate total love for Him. God is calling us back to Him.

Just as night and day cannot coexist, the worship of God cannot coexist with worship of any other sort. God wants us to worship Him and Him only. There is no in-between with God. He is not interested in sharing us. He refuses to be second. God is calling us to repent and turn back to Him and Get It Before It Gets You! Choose this day to let go of your It and allow God to take His rightful place in your life.

Journal

Do you have any Gomer characteristics when it comes to your relationship with God?

Have you ever been the victim of unfaithfulness? If so how did it make you feel?

Do you expect your spouse to be faithful to you and are you faithful to God?

What is your **It** and are you ready to let **It** go?

About the Author

Kelly L Shaw is the author of Preparing For God's Choosing "Spiritual Boot Camp, "she is married and the mother of 5 children. Kelly continues to fulfill her life purpose of equipping women of all ages, with the necessary tools to obtain freedom from bondage to a life of abundance through the power of Jesus Christ. Kelly enjoys reading God's Word and sharing God's Word through the art of dramatic interpretations. Kelly also loves fellowshipping with friends and family and spending quality time with her husband.

Contact:
The Author
Kelly L Shaw
www.kellyshawministries.com
kellyshawministries@gmail.com

HOLAM BOOKS & MEDIA
www.holambooks.com

Holam (חוֹלָם) is a Hebrew niqqud vowel sign represented by a dot above the upper left corner of the consonant letter. For example, here the holam appears after the letter mem (מ): מֹ. In Modern Hebrew it indicates the close-mid back rounded vowel, and is transliterated as an "o".